—*America*

LIVING FAITH
DAY BY DAY

How the Sacred Rules
of Monastic Traditions Can Help You Live
Spirituelly in the Modern World

*How the Sacred Rules
of Monastic Traditions Can Help You Live
Spiritually in the Modern World*

DEBRA K. FARRINGTON

A Perigee Book

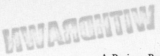

A Perigee Book
Published by The Berkley Publishing Group
A division of Penguin Putnam Inc.
375 Hudson Street
New York, New York 10014

First edition: August 2000

Published simultaneously in Canada.

The Penguin Putnam Inc. World Wide Web site address is
http://www.penguinputnam.com

Library of Congress Cataloging-in-Publication Data

Farrington, Debra K.
    Living faith day by day : how the sacred rules of monastic traditions can help you live spiritually in the modern world / Debra K. Farrington.
    p. cm.
    ISBN 0-399-52620-X
    1. Spiritual life—Christianity. 2. Monastic and religious life. I. Title.

BV4501.2.F327 2000
248.4—dc21   00-036719

Printed in the United States of America

10 9 8 7 6 5 4 3 2 1

For Joe and Rebecca, who continue to teach me how to live a rule of life, and for Val and Phyllis, for their unflagging support

Contents

PART ONE

What Is a Rule of Life?

CHAPTER ONE

The Invitation

"Listen carefully, my son, to the master's instructions,
and attend to them with the ear of your heart."

So begins the Rule of Life—St. Benedict's—that remains
the most widely known of monastic rules. The riches of
The Rule of St. Benedict have been mined by scholars, monks
and nuns, and laypeople for nearly fifteen centuries now, and
The Rule of St. Benedict continues to instruct and guide many
of us today. But Benedict's rule was written centuries after
many other ones, and was derivative of many other rules that
existed in Benedict's day. His rule—the guidelines by which
people in religious communities live—is only one of a variety
of ancient rules, and was not even particularly well-known
when it was written. While we gratefully look to the riches
of his work today, there are other rules, particularly the ones
from the fourth-century Egyptian desert monastics, as well
as ones written in today's monasteries, on which we can
draw with equal profit. Whether we live inside or outside of
religious enclosures, the monastic concept of balancing our

3

lives and ordering them around God offers hope for living a deeper and more fulfilling spiritual life.

Consider this book your invitation to create your own rule of life, one uniquely suited to you. A rule of life (though the word is singular) is actually a collection of rules or guidelines for living. These guidelines cover all aspects of our lives, and they help us to keep our lives in balance. Even more than that, however, a rule of life helps us to put and keep God at the center of everything we do. We do not strive for balance just for its own sake—though that is always pleasant. We create a balanced life so that we have time for our relationship with God. When we are too busy with our jobs, when we ignore the needs of our bodies or souls, we become focused solely on what we need or what is important to us. We lose track of what is important for others, for the world as a whole, and for God. We become disconnected from all that is around us and lose perspective. And, in the end, if we maintain this imbalance, we lose track of our relationship with God.

You may be balking at the world "rule" and perhaps there is good reason to bristle. The word can bring up childhood images of punishment and shame for some people. It can be hard to imagine that a rule might bring you great joy and peace. So while I use the term *rule of life* here, since it is a term out of the Christian heritage, substitute a more helpful term if you prefer. Perhaps you can think of the rule as a *way of life*.

One way to understand the importance of a rule is to think of it as you would a friendship in your life. Sometimes when we meet a new friend or a new romantic partner we ignore those who have been friends with us for a long time. We can do that for a little while without too much damage to the older friendships, but we cannot maintain that imbalance for long without risking attachments that are important to us. With our close friends and those who matter most to us, we find ways of relating to each other that work for everyone. Perhaps we call and talk to each other on the phone daily. Or we e-mail one another every week. Maybe we meet for a drink and conversation every Tuesday after work. We establish some sort of relationship—the regularity of it can vary enormously. But we have some mutually understood, even unconscious, way of staying connected. And as a result of the connection we grow and change, and our friend is transformed as well.

So it is with our connection to God. We must give time to the relationship. We must be present at some more or less regular interval. When we ignore it, or give insufficient time to it, God does not go away, but our mutual connection is weakened. When we pay attention, when we make time for God, as we do with friends and loved ones, we are challenged to grow and become more of what God intends for us. We fall in love with God over and over again, and we are richer for the experience.

That desire to be in a relationship with God is at the core of the rule of life. By making a commitment to prayer, to study, to a spiritual community, to our own needs and those of others, we create a balanced life that revolves around our love of God. We come to that commitment as a result of our own romance with God, out of the knowledge that God loves us and wants—desperately—to be in a relationship with us. And as a result of the love we experience we are emboldened and spread that love outward to others.

Before working specifically on developing your rule, it may be helpful to learn a bit about the history of the development of rules, for the struggles you probably face in living a life centered on God—while they may be new to you—are not new to humankind.

A Brief History of Rules

Pachomius and Basil

The struggle to find a way to live that is faithful to God no doubt began when people first began to experience God's presence. We cannot know anything of those earliest moments that occurred long before people began recording history, but the Bible and all the ancient documents from the early Jewish and Christian eras tell us of people's struggle to understand God, and to live somehow as they thought God required. Whole books of the Bible, such as Leviticus, document the human search to live according to what was perceived as divine will.

Our exploration, however, begins at the end of the third century C.E. in Egypt and Palestine, when Christian monasticism made its first appearance.[1] Beginning around this time hermits made their way into the deserts to seek God in solitude. (The word *monk* comes from a Greek word that means *alone*.) These hermits or solitaries, both men and women, sought a total withdrawal from all worldly life in the desert. They renounced marriage, family, the normal comforts of life, and all possessions in order to free themselves from anything that distracted them from God.[2] Many desert dwellers became the famous holy people of their times, and their spiritual advice was avidly sought.

The monasticism of this time followed two distinct and different paths. The first group, the true hermits, went off into the desert and lived in caves out of sight and earshot of others. They were loosely organized into communities called lauras. At the center of the community of caves were some common buildings where the solitaries met on Sundays for worship and a shared meal. The central buildings also provided housing for guests as needed. But the majority of the hermit's time was spent alone, and each person was his or her own spiritual guide. The spiritual practices for these hermits focused primarily on quelling the body's needs since they believed that the body served only to distract one from God. Fasting, sleep deprivation, and all sorts of bodily mortification were common for the desert dwellers. And though it was not true of all the hermits, in some areas a competitive asceticism developed, with monks trying to deprive their bodies more seriously than the next monk, thus proving that the one who could stand the most punishment was closest to God.

The second group of monks during this time recognized the dangers of the solitary life followed by the hermits and formed monastic communities instead. The originator of these kinds of communities is said to be Pachomius, who was born in Egypt around 292 and died in 346. Pachomius founded the first monastic community alongside the upper Nile in Egypt and his rule for living within that community is the first rule we know of today. His monasteries attracted thousands of Christians, both men and women, who gathered to live in community together. Each monastery featured smaller houses in which dwelled twenty monks under the direction of the housemaster, who was also the group's spiritual guide. A cycle of daily prayer was practiced, and work was strongly encouraged not only as a means to support the monastery, but as a spiritual discipline. Almost every activity outlined in Pachomius's rule is subject to the observation or guidance of the housemaster for each community, in direct opposition to the life of the hermits.

Pachomius's rule and the community life that it fostered

strongly influenced another early founder of monastic communities, St. Basil, who over time came to be regarded as the father of Orthodox monasticism. Early in his life, around 357–58, Basil went to Egypt in search of a spiritual director, and came into contact with Pachomius's monasteries. When he returned home, Basil tried to live the solitary life for a few years, but perhaps as a result of his contact with Pachomian monasteries, decided that community life was superior to a totally solitary life. Basil founded a community in Caesarea, and wrote what are called today his Long Rules and Short Rules to guide that community, and the communities that followed it.

Unlike many of the rules that we have from the earliest days, which are detailed instructions on how to set up a community and govern its life, Basil's rules are more like essays about the spiritual life, and many parts of them seem very contemporary today. Basil was particularly disdainful of life lived in solitary because it fostered arrogant behavior—the kinds of competitive spiritual feats of some of the desert monastics—and because it provided no opportunity to learn spiritual practices such as humility and patience. Perhaps most important to Basil, living alone in a desert cave, isolated from others, gave one little opportunity to practice the commandment to love one's neighbor, and provided few if any outlets to practice charity toward others.

Basil's communities, then, practiced a more moderate spirituality, and the monks looked to their superiors for their particular spiritual practices. Harsh and harmful bodily practices were not encouraged, being viewed as extreme acts of willful individualism rather than as pathways to God. Work, on the other hand, was encouraged, just as it was in Pachomius's monasteries. It was seen as a way of supporting the community, perfecting the soul, and providing help for the poor.

Pachomius's and Basil's rules became the formative documents for many of the rules that followed. What is perhaps the most fascinating aspect about them is that these two rules developed in response to a spiritual trend of third-century Christians that bears a remarkable similarity to today's spiritual dilemmas. During the 1970s and 1980s in America many individuals sought to create and direct their own spiritual paths. They fled from institutional religion and tried to direct their own spiritual searches much as the desert hermits did in third- and fourth-century Egypt. These hermits, acting as their own spiritual guides, were easily led to excesses and misdirection. The less spiritually hardy of them found themselves in competition with other monks, trying to outdo others in self-mortification, rather than truly following the pathway to God. Because they lived outside community there was no one to tell them they were on the wrong road, no one to make alternate suggestions for the journey. With only the self to think about, many of them did just that, and mistakenly focused on themselves when they thought they were focusing on God. Many contemporary spiritual seekers, trying to be their own guide, have discovered what the desert hermits found—that it is difficult to seek God alone and without help. The rules of Pachomius and Basil were important correctives in their time, and continue to be so today.

Later Rules: John Cassian, the Celts, and Benedict

The literature of the early monastic movement in the East attracted many spiritual seekers from the West who came and studied, and then brought monasticism back to what is now Europe. In the year 385 John Cassian went to Egypt in search of spiritual enlightenment, and studied at the feet of many of the great spiritual masters there. A theological controversy eventually drove him out of Egypt, and he settled in Gaul (what is now the western European continent, minus Spain) and there recorded the wisdom of the Eastern masters. Cassian's *Institutes*, which he wrote for a community of monks he helped to form in Provence, was the first rule to be produced in western Europe. Cassian believed that the solitary life was perhaps the highest form of spiritual achievement for a Christian, but like Pachomius and Basil he found it necessary for men and women to prepare themselves for the solitary search for God through spiritual formation with a structured community.

As monasticism spread throughout the West many new rules were created. The first half of the sixth century was a rich time for the development of rules, with new ones springing up regularly. Each was derivative of what had already been written by previous writers; such a practice was considered one that gave honor to earlier authors, rather than as plagiarism. In Italy and southern Gaul two rules developed that influenced what is probably the best known rule today, The Rule of St. Benedict. Though there is scholarly disagreement about this, some scholars believe that *The Rule of the Master*, written by an unknown abbot, was written at the beginning of the sixth century. Borrowing from *The Rule of the Master*, St. Caesarius of Arles (c. 470–542) wrote two rules, one for men and one for women. St. Benedict (c. 480–550) in turn, drew heavily on both of these sources for his now famous rule. Written in a more organized fashion and a more literary style, and memorialized by Pope Gregory the Great in his *Life of St. Benedict*, written about 593–4, Benedict's rule become the one that influenced much of what would come after him.

In comparison to many of the other rules of his day, Benedict's is less harsh and autocratic than most. The abbot, in Benedict's rule, is required to consult with the whole community, and the questioning of authority—within certain boundaries—is even allowed. Benedict's rule is not one that asks for excessively harsh treatment of the body either, though none of the early rules encouraged any coddling of bodily needs. But Benedict's rule makes provisions for those who are sick and innately weaker than others, asking each person to perform at the level at which he is reasonably capable, and not to compare himself to others.

Alongside the development of monasteries and rules in the West came the same process in Ireland. Perhaps as early as the fifth century, but certainly in the sixth century, monasticism spread throughout Ireland. Scholars are agreed that Irish monasticism was influenced by what had come before it, but are not sure whether this came from contact with the West or possibly from direct contact with the East. The first Irish rule we know of is that of St. Columbanus. His rule and many of the other Celtic rules that followed show a different side of Celtic life than the one often portrayed in popular books today. Like their counterparts in the Egyptian desert, the Irish rules focused on conquering the body in order to bring the soul to God.[3] It is not unusual to find, in some of these rules, instructions to do something like genuflecting 100 times a day—an activity that would quickly destroy the cartilage in anyone's knees. As another example, the following passage comes from Columbanus' rule: "The chief part of the monk's rule is mortification . . . Let the monk . . . not do as he wishes, let him eat what is bidden, keep as much as he has received, complete the tale of his work, be subject to him whom he does not like. Let him come wearily as if sleep-walking to bed, and let him be forced to rise while his sleep is not yet finished."[4]

Columbanus' rule, however, spread over to Gaul and was very popular for a period of time. In fact, some monastic houses combined the rules of Columbanus and Benedict, and lived what they called a "mixed rule." Eventually, however, given the harshness of the Celtic rules, Benedict's rule became the preferred model, and was adopted as the sole rule for many monasteries.

Another well-known rule is The Rule of St. Augustine, which became the basic rule of the Dominican Order in the Catholic Church. Briefer than most rules, and much more general in its instruction, it focuses on poverty, simplicity, and obedience. Like the rules of Basil and Pachomius, it stresses the importance of living together in community: "Before all else, *live together in harmony* [Psalm 67 (68):7], being *of one mind and one heart* [Acts 4:32] on the way to God. For is it not precisely for this reason that you have come together?"

There is no need to explore the complete history of rules here, nor has that history ended—rules are being written and revised even today. Many of the ancient rules were living documents in their times, repeatedly revised by their authors and the authors' successors. That remains true even today. Monasteries and convents may still use Benedict's rule, but they reinterpret it for today's world. The Rule of the Society of St. John the Evangelist, a more contemporary community of monks, was first written in 1866, and was recently revised again.[5] By their nature rules are living documents, and are rewritten and reassessed in light of what the author or succeeding generations learn of God.

Rules for Individuals

So far we have explored the rules that were written for monastic communities, but increasingly in the last few years spiritual directors and seekers are paying attention to the application of rules to the lives of individuals. The wide variety of commentaries on The Rule of St. Benedict in recent years has helped individuals see that rules can provide guidance and help shape their personal religious journey, just as they do for an individual within a community. In fact, most rules would encourage individuals to form some kind of religious community, even if it is only a relationship with one other person, such as a spiritual director. In the last ten years or so a variety of books containing ancient rules have been published, and you will find many of them listed on pages 269–76. At the same time, a small number of spiritual writers have devoted a chapter or two in their books to rules, suggesting that individuals discern a rule of life tailored to their own life and experience of God. "When people come to me for spiritual direction," Margaret Guenther writes, "I always assume that, at some level, they are concerned with formulating a rule of life. They may not use these words . . . But they are concerned with the stewardship of their time and energy (as well as their substance) and are looking for help in shaping their days."[6] Guenther, a spiritual director, goes on to point out that we are all living a rule of life, but that for most of us this rule is unconscious.

To discover elements of your own unconscious rule of life, try the following exercise.[7] Your answers to the exercise will form the groundwork for any rule you create for yourself as you read through the remainder of the book. So, before reading any further, take a few moments and make a list of all the things that you currently do that nurture your spirit.

Make the list as complete as possible, coming back to it over the next few days if need be. Write down everything you do that nurtures your spirit, and try to avoid censoring anything you might put on the list.

Now, what do you notice about your list? When people think of activities that are spiritual, they normally only consider things such as prayer, worship, meditation, and other activities associated with spirituality. Some of those may well appear on your list, but in all likelihood it probably included many items outside those parameters, because I asked you what nurtures your spirit, rather than your spiritual life. Are there things on the list that surprise you? For instance, maybe you put a hobby (quilting, gardening, carpentry) on your list and never thought about it before as something spiritually nurturing. Are there people on your list who nurture your soul? How do they do that? For some people, activities such as long, intimate conversations, or making love, appear on their lists. Does what you do for a living appear anywhere? Try to notice what is not on your list as well as what appears there. As you try to think about the things on your list, be sure to add anything else that comes to mind.

Congratulations! You now have a large part of the work done on developing your own rule of life. These are things you are already doing that connect your spiritual life with your daily life, activities in which God is already present. You have a basic rule of life already, even if it has been unconscious up until now, and knowing that will help you to continue practicing your rule consciously. You may, however, have noticed that some parts of your life are missing from the rule. Perhaps nothing in your job feels spiritually nurturing. Maybe you have no time for prayer or quiet. For now, simply notice what is missing and don't worry too much about it. As you continue reading through this book look for suggestions, particularly in the second part of the book, about ways you might fill in the blanks.

The remainder of this book will help you uncover the rule you are already keeping and add to your rule so that it encompasses as many aspects of your life as possible. Chapter 2 provides guidance on how to establish, keep, and regularly evaluate your rule. The eight chapters in the second part of this book look at specific areas I suggest you address in forming your rule of life: seeking God, rules that focus on your prayer life, work, study of God, spiritual companionship and worship community, care of your body, reaching out to care for others, and offering hospitality. Each chapter in part two includes a variety of suggestions for rules in a given area, all of them on the wisdom of ancient or contemporary rules. Like all good rules, the one you ultimately set will benefit from the wisdom of rules that have already been written. In order to be sure that your rule covers all aspects of your life, try to pick at least one of the suggested rules from each chapter, or use something similar that comes to mind while you are reading.

I hope you will discover, in the process of establishing and keeping a rule, that it opens up an ever-deepening conversation with God that enriches your own life, and allows you, in turn, to be the presence of God to everything that exists around you.

CHAPTER TWO

Discovering a Rule You Can Live With

"When someone comes to the door of the monastery, wishing to renounce the world and be added to the number of the brothers, he shall not be free to enter. . . . He shall remain outside at the door for a few days and be taught the Lord's Prayer and as many Psalms as he can learn. Carefully shall he make himself known: Has he done something wrong and, troubled by fear, suddenly run away? Or is he under someone's authority? . . . If they see that he is ready for everything, then he shall be taught the rest of the monastic discipline."

—The Rule of Pachomius

Perhaps, by now, the idea of developing a rule of life reminds you of one of our annual events—the declaration of our New Year's resolutions. Every year around December 31st we turn our attention to our resolutions as local news shows interview people on the street proclaiming their resolution this year to lose weight, to exercise more, to study harder, to be nicer to their friends and family, or whatever else comes to mind. Most of us, when we make these promises, intend to keep them, and we do—for a week or two. Gyms and diet programs feature all sorts of specials and sign up lots of new members in January, but their facilities are back to normal come February. We mean well with our New Year's resolutions, but the breaking of them is as much an annual tradition as establishing them in the first place.

New Year's resolutions, as well-intentioned as they may be, rarely become a significant part of our life. We usually think them through and commit ourselves to them out of a sense of inadequacy: We are too fat, too slothful, not smart enough, not nice enough. So we set ourselves goals of being skinnier, more energetic, nicer, brighter, and when that turns out to be unattainable in two weeks' time, we give up. Rather than helping us connect to something greater than ourselves, and rather than helping us discover that we are loved as we are, New Year's resolutions tend to reinforce our self-centeredness and our negative self-images. They probably do us more harm than good, for they remind us year after year that we continue to be unacceptable because we are still too fat, too ugly, too stupid, and not popular enough. New Year's resolutions more often drag us down than build us up.

A rule of life, however, is not a New Year's resolution, and we approach it from a very different perspective. A personal rule of life is a response, first and foremost, to the God who loves us more than we will ever completely understand. It helps us to make God the focus of every activity and thought in our life. We choose to pray not because it calms us (though it may well do that) but because prayer brings us into a relationship with what is holy, and that contact nurtures our bodies, minds, and souls. We choose to study because by examining the thoughts and words of others we will know God more fully. We care for and honor our bodies not to win beauty contests, but because God has entrusted the stewardship of this body to us for now, and it deserves our care as do all other parts of creation.

The creation and observance of a rule of life comes about as we begin to experience God and yearn for a more intimate relationship; it is a response born out of affection or love and desire. Just as Pachomius's rule, quoted above, advises those in the monastery to admit only new members who come for the right reasons—who are not running away from, but running toward God—we, too, come to a rule of life out of desire and not fear. When we discern and practice our rule from a place of affection, our relationship and knowledge of God deepens. And as the relationship becomes more central in our life, keeping the rule itself assumes more importance and becomes a vehicle for deepening our relationship not only to God, but to ourselves and to the rest of creation. A rule of life, then, may very well help us to feel better about ourselves, but it does so because it opens up God's unconditional love to us. In discovering that we are loved exactly as we are, we become free to grow, change, and develop from a positive place rather than from a negative or self-destructive one.

Rules differ from New Year's resolutions in another way: They are not created in a moment, or even in a couple of days at the end of December. Rules must be discovered over a period of time, and they must be allowed to grow and evolve. The rules we read in books today, such as Benedict's rule and others, give the false impression that each was written all at one time, but that is not the case. The ancient rules that we have access to today were constantly evolving documents. Historians and religious scholars can trace the inconsistencies of language and thought within the documents themselves that prove that they were constantly amended and rethought before being put in the form we have now. Some of the rules even appear to have been revised by people other than the original author. Contemporary rules, too, receive regular reviews within their communities. The recently published The Rule of the Society of St. John the Evangelist, for instance, even includes an interesting chapter on how their current rule was rethought and amended over a period of eight years. Rules, then, are living documents. They take time to uncover in the first place, and a good rule evolves as you grow and change.

Just as a rule of life does not evolve in a day, neither will you find yourself expert at keeping a rule overnight. Here are some helpful tips for living with your rule:

1. Listen to your heart's desires. God often speaks to us through our heart's desires.

2. Make sure your rule includes some joy, play, and fun.

3. Take baby steps. Don't make your rule too hard to follow.

4. Baby steps are good, but give yourself a little bit of challenge, too.

5. Figure out how much structure you need: lots or just a little?

6. Learn to pay attention deeply to your practices. It will help prevent boredom.

7. Find someone to talk with about your rule; it is easy to fool ourselves about all sorts of things.

8. Figure out how to help yourself be accountable for keeping your rule.

9. Read your rule regularly. It's easy to forget the stuff we don't like so much.

10. You're going to have trouble keeping a rule sometimes. Recognize that you're human, and try again.

Discovering Your Personal Rule of Life

Two things are important to consider in setting a rule for yourself: paying attention to your heart's desires and being realistic. Taking both of these into account through prayer, meditation, and conversation with others, and using both of them to discern your rule, will help you develop a rule you can live with for a lifetime.

God often speaks to us through the deepest desires of our hearts. People frequently discover the real work that God intends for them by paying attention to the kinds of tasks or activities that seem to bring them into close contact with what is holy. The same is true for prayer styles, study, and the other categories outlined in part two of this book. For instance, I loved to write as a child, but left that activity behind as I grew up. As an adult, a colleague of mine decided I needed to be writing, and she set some wheels in motion that have resulted in continuous writing for many years now. Writing—something I felt called to and ignored—turns out to be praying for me. When I am not writing, the other areas of my life suffer as well. By paying attention to my heart's desire I discovered a way of praying that brings me into contact with what is sacred.

But not all of this need be such serious work. Children

seem to be in touch with the joy and wonder of life—with God—when they are playing. As adults we often forget that a life in tune with God is often a joyful one, even when personal circumstances make life difficult. Often, when our hearts desire laughter and joy, we forget that these gifts from God open us to the presence of God in ourselves and in others. Some of the people I would count as most holy in this life also laugh easily and fully, and they delight in life. I had the opportunity to listen to the Dalai Lama speak once, for instance, and was entranced by his presentation. But what struck me most was that at the end of his talk he turned to the audience and asked us to take anything useful from what he had said and live that fully, or, if we had found nothing of value in the conversation, we should just forget it and move on. The audience roared with laughter, partly because of the absurdity and humility of such a holy man suggesting that he had nothing useful to offer us. The ability to take oneself lightly, to be playful and funny, is as much a part of being in touch with God as are activities we would normally consider more serious. It is important, then, to pay attention to all of our heart's desires, and not just those ones we normally associate with holy or sacred behavior.

That is why, in the exercise in chapter 1, you were asked to name those activities that nurture your spirit, rather than your spiritual life. We too often limit our understanding of the spiritual life to activities that have traditionally been defined as prayer, worship, and perhaps the study of Scriptures. But all things that nurture the spirit feed the spiritual life. Gardening, if it gives you meditative time that connects you with creation and the wonder of what God has given us, can be a deeply spiritual experience. It can lead us to a deeper connection to what is sacred when through it we find time to be with God, or when we discover that the earth needs our care and we put our energies into the careful stewardship of the environment. If gardening is one of the things that your heart desires the most, then make that a part of your rule of life.

While following our heart's desires can lead us to God, there are also times when doing so leads us away from anything holy and sacred. We are human beings, and we have a great capacity to fool ourselves. Not long ago the nightly television news featured a murderer who had dreamt all his life of killing women, and he finally acted on that deepest desire. While we must be aware of our hopes and dreams, and may want to incorporate them into our rule of life, we will need to test them by looking for affirmation of their value and worth in other previously written rules, or by discussing them with a trusted friend or spiritual director.

Constructing a rule that consists only of our heart's desires needs to be avoided as well. A rule of life helps us grow closer to God not only through activities and practices that speak to us right this moment, but by helping us to stretch and grow in areas where we are less mature. Many of us, for instance, see few connections between care of our body and a deeper relationship with God. Many of the ancient rules reinforce this separation, as Christianity has traditionally had a difficult time viewing the body as a gift from God, rather than as an obstacle to being fully present with God. This has been changing in recent decades, and contemporary rules frequently view the body's physical needs in a positive rather than a negative way, but most of us live with centuries' worth of old baggage on this score. Consequently, whether your heart desires to attend to your own physical needs or not, this needs to be included in your rule as one of the ways of growing in your understanding of and relationship to God.

Ancient and contemporary rules all have different aspects

on which they focus, and there is not a final, definitive list of categories for rules. This book offers eight generally accepted categories for your consideration—ones that are most often addressed in monastic rules. In order to form a balanced rule that helps your current spiritual practices grow and stretches you, I would encourage you to pick a practice or an attitude in each of the eight areas. Briefly they are the following:

1. The Foundations: putting God at the center of your rule and your life;

2. Prayer: finding a prayer type and rhythm that works for you;

3. Work: approaching your work as part of your spiritual life, rather than something divorced from it;

4. Study: establishing a regular practice of learning more about God;

5. Spiritual companionship: committing yourself to regular companionship and community on the journey;

6. Care of your body: taking care of yourself as a spiritual practice;

7. Reaching out: caring for others and the environment as a spiritual practice;

8. Hospitality: finding ways to be a gracious presence in the world.

With these eight categories in mind, take the list you made in chapter 1 and plug the items on that list into the eight areas. Notice particularly any categories in which nothing appears. As you read through part two of the book, which focuses on specific suggestions in each of these areas, add to or subtract from your basic rule as appropriate. Pay particular attention to the suggestions in chapters that focus on categories in which you have not listed anything that nurtures you right now, and try to commit to one of the suggestions given, or to something else that comes to mind as a result of what you read. Don't try to read all the chapters in one day and discern your entire rule at once. As you consider each category give yourself some time to listen to your own heart, and to listen for God's call to you in that area.

Also pay attention to what is reasonable for your own schedule, lifestyle, and needs. Newcomers seeking to incorporate these practices into their lives often make the same mistake we all do with New Year's resolutions: They set themselves up for failure by committing to something more difficult than they can actually maintain. It is akin to going to the gym after being stationary for years and lifting weights that are too heavy for your untrained body. Usually that results in a very sore body, feelings of frustration and incompetence, and avoidance of the gym in the future.

The Secular Franciscans is a lay order of people attached to a monastic one, and all members of the Secular Franciscans commit to maintaining a rule of life. As they form their first personal rule, the order recommends that they set a reasonable rule, rather than taking on one appropriate to Mother Teresa. Spiritual life, and spiritual disciplines require practice to develop and maintain. You might only be able to lift a spiritual weight of three pounds today, but if you stay with the practice, pretty soon you'll be lifting five pounds, and then ten. In working with your rule, keep the practicalities of your lifestyle and needs in mind. If all you have right now is five minutes a day for prayer, it is far better to commit to those five minutes than to establish a rule about praying forty-five minutes a day and failing to keep that promise.

Before finalizing the rule it is advisable to talk with a trusted friend, pastor, or spiritual director who can help you see if the rule is balanced, reasonable, and one that you can maintain over a period of time. We can too easily fool ourselves by adopting a rule that is too challenging, not challenging enough, or one that leaves out important areas that don't appeal to us personally. We'll look a bit more closely at the role of a companion in discovering and keeping a rule a little later in this chapter.

How Much Structure Do You Need?

Many of the ancient rules, and even some of the contemporary ones, include very detailed descriptions of the various requirements of the rule: the specific hours for prayers, the exact number of Psalms to be read, the amount of bread to be eaten, the number of hours spent in reading, and hundreds of other details. Other rules, such as St. Augustine's, provide only broad guidelines that are subject to individual interpretation, rather than detailed schedules and procedures. How much structure you require in your rule is up to you; each of us operates differently.

Perhaps you are a person for whom a specific kind of rhythm to the day works well. A friend of mine, who loves the early morning, finds that her relationship to God is most fulfilling when she regularly reads her Bible and prays during the dawn hours when no one else in the house is up and about. She takes this same time to pray and study nearly every day, and finds the structure helpful. But I look at that kind of schedule and shudder even thinking about it. With my busy schedule and the amount of travel through various time zones I do, I cannot even imagine trying to carve out the same period of time each day. Still, my rule includes a commitment to regular prayer, and very rarely does a day pass without my taking some time for that, even if it is a few minutes. Just as my friend has discovered that structure deepens her relationship to God, I have discovered that being overly structured with my rule destroys my sense of God's presence.

You may have to experiment a bit to find out what works for you, and what you discover might even surprise you. My friend who loves a structured prayer life does not find the same need for structure in many other parts of her life. I am extremely methodical and organized in my work life, but loathe that type of structure in my spiritual life. If you are not sure what will work for you, make some of your rules general guidelines and some of them more detailed in their practice, and see how you feel about them after a few months. The rule you set should offer you some challenge and push you just a bit, but not be so structured or so unstructured that you find yourself unable to keep it.

In setting up a structure of some kind, a spiritual friend or advisor can prove invaluable. I spent several years trying to force myself to keep a very detailed rule, and ended up failing to keep it all too often. In conversation with my spiritual director, however, we realized that the structure and not the rule itself was the barrier to my spiritual life. Without the corroboration of my director, however, I would have felt less comfortable making my rule less specific. It is too hard for me to look at myself sometimes and know when I am being too hard on myself versus when I am simply not applying myself enough. The voice of someone who knows me and cares about my spiritual growth was invaluable in helping me to see clearly what was happening and make the needed adjustments.

Maintenance

If you are like me, you will probably enjoy the first few weeks of living your rule. The newness of the experience, the discoveries, and general enthusiasm will probably keep you going for a little while. But somewhere around two weeks or so into any new activity I have a tendency to get bored. I've gotten the gist of the exercise, had some good experiences with it, but now the infatuation period has worn off, and routine sets it. This is when keeping the rule gets difficult. But unless we are willing to move past the infatuation stage and begin to plumb the depths of what seems routine, we will never find true intimacy with God. Mountaintop experiences of God, like the excitement at the beginning of any spiritual practice, are all well and good, but they are not the stuff of which long-term relationships are made. Faithfulness to God is a long-term commitment, and only later, after much practice and attentiveness to your rule, will you be able to see where you have been and where you might be going.

Two strategies for dealing with boredom include providing variety and paying attention. When you are constructing your rule pay attention to the kinds of variety that you can build into it. For instance, if you commit yourself to regular exercise as a way of caring for your body, you may want to vary the types of exercises you do, the order in which you carry out the routines, or the place in which you do them. If reading is a part of your regular study practice, alternate between various books of the Bible, or read a wide variety of books—fiction and nonfiction. If you have a particular practice that does not allow for much variation, then try to teach yourself to pay attention to the details of the activity or your response to it. If, for instance, you have chosen to say a particular prayer or to meditate at a set time each day, practice listening very carefully to the words, or to the silence, and notice subtle changes in what you observe or hear. Nothing is ever the same from one time to the next, and paying attention at a deep level can help to prevent boredom.

I have mentioned already that a spiritual advisor of some sort is essential in helping you and challenging you on questions of discernment and structure. Spiritual directors and pastors can help you discover, adjust, and keep your rule. Or you might also choose to have a spiritual friend with whom to talk. A particularly helpful strategy might be to invite a friend you trust to develop his or her own rule as well, and then meet monthly to talk about how each of you is doing with your commitment. We get too close to ourselves sometimes, and do not always see things that others see. We can be blind to both positive and negative things about ourselves and our lives, and it takes a trusted friend or director to tell us the truth in a loving way. But these advisors can also be helpful in keeping us accountable for following our rule. When the press of daily schedules and other commitments crowd our lives, rules can disappear from our consciousness. A regular meeting with someone who will help us with our rule keeps us focused and accountable. When we slip we receive help in getting back on the path. When we are doing well with our rule, we receive affirmation. When things aren't working for a period of time, we can turn to our advisor for a new perspective. There have been many times in my life when my rule would have gone by the wayside without the help, support, and perspective of spiritual directors and friends, and even those trained in spiritual matters (such as spiritual directors and pastors) find that this is true.

In addition to a regular monthly conversation with someone, you may find it helpful to chart your progress on a daily basis. Again, this will be a matter of personal taste and finding what works most effectively for you. A friend of mine who finds the monthly conversations helpful tells me that the idea of tracking her rule on any more of a regular basis would drive her simply insane, and be a detriment to her spiritual life. Some people, however, particularly in the beginning while they are developing their rule, find it useful to keep a record of their commitments on a daily or weekly basis. When I was first trying to develop the habit of regular exercise, for instance, I found it useful to make a note in my personal calendar on each day I actually exercised. That way I could see how many times I had (or had not) exercised in a given week, and either give myself a pat on the back or recommit myself to getting back to the gym. Eventually I found that I did not need to do that anymore, but in the beginning the tracking helped me make this commitment.

Another friend of mine uses what she calls a "star chart" to help her stay focused on her rule. On a sheet of paper that she keeps on the refrigerator (since she lives alone) she has a grid on which she records the days of the week across the top, with her rules listed down the left-hand side. Every time she keeps one of her rules she puts a star in the appropriate box. Some might find this kind of system unworkable, but for my friend the star chart has pleasant childhood memories and she finds it fun.

Finally, reread your rule regularly. As St. Augustine writes: "This little book [the rule] is to be read to you once a week. As in a mirror, you will be able to see in it whether there is anything you are neglecting or forgetting." Some parts of your rule may not need daily or weekly attention, or there may be parts that you find more challenging and difficult.

These pieces can sometimes slip from your mind, and a regular reading of your rule will bring them back to your attention.

There will, of course, be times, when you fail to keep your rule. Whether you find yourself off track for a day or two, a week, or longer, it is never too late to start again. Dealing harshly with yourself rarely helps. We are human beings, and none of us is perfect. As you begin to recognize or deal with your temporary wander away from the rule, take some time to pray about that, to confess your shortcomings to God, and to recommit yourself to the rule. If you have a spiritual friend or advisor, talk with that person, too. Perhaps he or she can help you discover what it was that weakened your commitment temporarily, and provide some suggestions about avoiding that particular obstacle in the future.

Presuming that you spent some time discerning the rule you have set, and that you've prayed about it, and discussed it with others, try to keep that initial rule at least two months before you consider any changes to it. Others would suggest that six months or even a year is a more appropriate period for practicing your rule before making any changes, and giving it a longer period of time will help to ensure that you are not giving up any part of the rule simply because of boredom or a whim. But keep it for at least two months, and if you find that there are parts of the rule that are not working well—if you are simply not keeping one of the commitments or you find a particular practice unhelpful—then find out what needs to be changed. Your spiritual friend or advisor can be very useful, and can help you to discover if you need more or less structure or a different practice altogether. Unless the rule has been totally unworkable, try to make small changes to one or two areas, rather than rewriting the entire rule. A small adjustment in one aspect of your rule may affect other parts of it, and you will need time to observe what happens to the whole rule as you change portions of it.

Once you have determined your basic rule and you are keeping your commitment to it, try to take time annually to review what you are doing. A good rule helps us grow closer to God and to deepen our spiritual understandings, so it is natural to outgrow all or part of your rule at some point in time. Just as the original creators of ancient and contemporary rules tinkered with them as their own spiritual lives developed, so will you. An annual review, either privately or with your spiritual advisor, will help you to identify areas in which you have grown and may need to challenge yourself a bit more, and it will also help you see more clearly the path on which God leads you.

PART TWO

Living a Rule of Life

CHAPTER THREE

Seeking God

"You want to seek God with all your life, and love Him with all your heart . . . To choose God is to realize that you are known and loved in a way surpassing anything one can imagine, loved before anyone had thought of you or spoken your name."

—Rule for a New Brother

Rule for a New Brother begins with these words: "You want to seek God with all your life, and love Him with all your heart." More than anything else, that is what a rule of life is about—seeking and loving God. To live a rule of life is to choose God, and to place God at the center of your world, rather than focus on yourself. At the same time, the rule we establish helps us to seek God with every single part of our life, not just with prayer, but in all our relationships, in study, in play, in work, as well as in the care of ourselves and the world around us. There is no part of our life that is beyond God's reach. We choose to follow a rule because we have chosen God, and living a rule helps us to keep choosing God as the focus of every part of our life.

But in seeking God, we often come to recognize one of the paradoxes of the spiritual life—that God was there all along. What felt like the absence of God was our own absence from the relationship, not God's. "Where can I go from your spirit?" Psalm 139 asks. Or "where can I flee from your presence? If I ascend to heaven, you are there; if I make my bed in Sheol, you are there." The writer of the Psalm continues to name place after place, and God is in all of them. God may not demand our attention or insist on a relationship we do not want, but there is nowhere we can go that God is absent.

When we come to realize that God has been there all along, we also discover that we are loved deeply and unconditionally. Otherwise, why would God stay with us, despite our obvious faults? A popular television show reminds viewers of this message week after week. The plot varies from show to show, but the message is identical in every episode. The character who has been in crisis throughout the week's story is confronted by an angel who reminds him or her that God loves them, no matter what has happened. The shows are almost perfect templates of one another: They vary only in minor details. But it captures a large viewing audience each week because the message of God's love is so powerful, and we seem to need reminding that God loves us no matter what.

It is the simplest message in the world, and perhaps one of the most difficult for many of us to truly believe. Once we catch a glimmer of that truth, however, we respond by seeking God even more. The process is not unlike falling in love with another person. We catch a glimmer of God somewhere in our lives and form some sort of relationship. As time goes on we work through whatever issues arise, we enjoy the companionship, and we grow more attached to the relationship.

One day we realize that we are in love, and that only makes us want to be closer to God. The seeking leads to love, which leads to seeking, and so on. The deeper in love with God we are the more we understand that God loves everything and everyone around us, just as he loves us, and we begin to seek God in all creation, and to fall in love with God's presence everywhere.

That is why Rule for a New Brother—as well as all other rules, explicitly or implicitly—begins with seeking God. Without that desire, the spiritual life withers and dies. We may be angry with God or hate something for which we blame God, but that need not prevent us from seeking God and demanding explanations. It is that desire—even demand—to find meaning, to ask God why we are here and what life is about, to be in relationship with God who is more than we can possibly imagine, that drives us into God's arms finally. One of the most lyrical expressions of the desire for God in the various rules can be found in The Earlier Rule of St. Francis. Most of his rule is written in prose, but near the end he breaks into poetry:

> 9. Therefore
> let us desire nothing else
> let us wish for nothing else
> let nothing else please us
> and cause us delight
> except our Creator and Redeemer and Savior,
> the one true God,
> Who is the Fullness of Good,
> all good, every good, the true and supreme good
> Who alone is Good
> merciful and gently
> delectable and sweet

Who alone is holy
just and true
holy and right
Who alone is kind
innocent
pure
from Whom and through Whom and in Whom is
all pardon
all grace
all glory
of all of the penitent and the just
of all the blessed who rejoice together in heaven.

10. Therefore
let nothing hinder us
nothing separate us
or nothing come between us.

11. Let all of us
wherever we are
in every place
at every hour
every day and continually
believe truly and continually
believe truly and humbly
and keep in [our] heart
and love, honor, adore, serve
praise and bless
glorify and exalt
magnify and give thanks to
the most high and supreme eternal God
Trinity and Unity
the Father and the Son and the Holy Spirit

Creator of all
Savior of all who believe in Him
and Hope in Him
and love Him
Who is
without beginning and without end
unchangeable, invisible,
indescribable, ineffable,
incomprehensible, unfathomable,
blessed, worth of praise,
glorious, exalted on high, sublime,
most high, gentle, lovable,
delectable and totally desirable above all else
forever.
Amen.[8]

So, like Francis, seek God with all your life, in everything you do, and everyone you meet. Choose God, and experience love beyond measure.

The rules in this foundation chapter all address facets of our process of seeking God, and all are implied in any rule of life that exists. As you continue to read through the remaining chapters in part two of this book, pay attention to the rules that will help you make God the focus of all you do. Look for and choose to practice those rules that help you make God a part of the workplace, your home life, your relationships, your prayer life, and everything else that fills your days.

Bring Everything to God

"The hermit listens to his feelings, desires, needs, motives, attitudes . . . In dealing honestly with all of these, he comes to God as a human being with emotions . . . that need healing . . . Recognizing one's own needs, whether intellectual, physical, emotional, or spiritual, will make one more aware of the needs of others."

—Hermits of Bethlehem

Some years ago, when I worked in a bookstore, one of my favorite titles was *May I Hate God?* That tiny little book posed a question many of us are afraid to ask. The answer in the book was "Yes, you may hate God. God can take it." Maybe I liked the title so much because at a difficult time in my life all I could think of to say to God was "Where the hell were you when bad things were happening in my life? Why me?" That was my most regular prayer for quite a while and it was also my pathway to a deeper relationship with God. Perhaps our relationship with God is like our relationship with anyone we care about: If we are not honest with the other person concerning our feelings, desires, and needs, then the relationship withers and perhaps it dies. It is, however, more difficult to bring all of ourselves to another person than to God, since we run the risk of being rejected by people we care about. With God that possibility disappears. God already knows everything we are thinking and feeling, so we can be as angry or sad or guilty as we wish and still God will be present and continue to love us.

If you don't believe this is true, you might spend some time reading the Book of Psalms in the Bible. The Psalms are prayers or poems spoken directly to God, for the most part, and they contain every emotion you or I have ever experienced. Some of the Psalms strike us as very unpleasant and are filled with angry, whiney, and difficult people. In the Psalms we find people filled with hatred, who beg God to bring violent and painful destruction on the writer's enemies. Many of the writers make self-righteous and arrogant statements, vilifying others as evil, and glorifying those who obey God. Through human eyes, God is portrayed as vengeful, full of wrath, and quick to punish.

Others writers express deep sorrow; they are destitute and find no relief in sight. "I am weary with my moaning; every night I flood my bed with tears; I drench my couch with my weeping." (Psalm 6:6) The Psalm writers beg for mercy, even almost bribing God on occasion. "Turn, O Lord, save my life; deliver me for the sake of your steadfast love. For in death there is no remembrance of you; in Sheol who can give you praise?" (Psalm 6:4–5)

More to our contemporary tastes are the Psalms that are love songs to God. The beginning of Psalm 23, familiar to anyone who went through a few years of church school, still speaks to our hearts: "The Lord is my shepherd, I shall not want." Or try the exalted beginning of Psalm 84: "How lovely is your dwelling place, O Lord of Hosts! My soul longs, indeed it faints for the courts of the Lord; my heart and my flesh sing for joy to the living God." (Psalm 84:1–2)

If you read through the whole book of Psalms you will discover that there is not a single emotion, need, or desire that has not already been brought before God. You cannot possibly surprise God with anything you have to say; God has already seen and heard it all. While we may be horrified by some of the more vicious Psalms, we can also take comfort in knowing that others have been as hateful and mean-spirited as we are at times. The same is true for our sorrows and our joys. Not only has God seen and heard it all, but God delights in each of us as we are and never grows weary of our conversation with him.

So we bring all our intellectual, physical, emotional, and spiritual needs to God, and in doing so, deepen that relationship. We will begin to understand how deeply God loves us, and how deeply God must love everything else as well. In finding all of our own needs acceptable in God's sight, we can begin to be aware of the needs of others that God also finds acceptable. The purpose of bringing everything to God is not a purely individualistic or narcissistic practice in the end; it is about being aware of the needs of others as well, and learning to make provision for them in our daily interactions. We deepen our relationship with God in order to fill the internal reservoirs that allow us to be the presence of God in the lives of others.

Practice

1. Make a list of all the intellectual, physical, emotional, or spiritual needs that you deliberately avoid

bringing to God. Be as honest as you can with yourself.

2. Now read through the book of Psalms in the Bible. Make a mark in your Bible or make a list of the Psalms you like, for whatever reason. Now make a mark by the Psalms or make a list of Psalms that express anger, sorrow, fearfulness, and joy. For example, Psalm 84 expresses joy.

3. From your list, match the issues that you do not feel you can bring to God with a Psalm that speaks to the same or similar feelings. For instance, if you do not feel that you can bring your anger to God, take a look at Psalm 43. Use the Psalm or Psalms you find as your prayer for these needs until you are ready to speak to God more directly about what concerns you.

Give Thanks

"As soon as everything that is done at table is finished, all rise as the abbot does so, and the whole community says along with the servers and the cellerer, 'Thanks be to God!' "

—The Rule of the Master

I worked with an author once who taught me a great deal about being grateful. The whole time we worked together he was dying from a genetic disease that had already killed all his siblings. He had lived a good deal longer than many other people with his disease and I was fortunate to know him, even if it was only for the last nine months of his life. I don't believe Bill ever ended a conversation with me without thanking me for publishing his book. About two weeks before he died, Bill called me and spent a whole hour telling me how blessed his life had been and how grateful he was for everything he had been given. I listened to him tell me about how much he valued his wife, the time he had spent in seminary, and all the people he had met there, how thankful he was for seeing his book in print before he died, and much more. It was our last conversation and I knew it when we talked. Bill was calling to say good-bye and he needed someone to listen to him tell his story once again before dying. I think I was in tears the entire hour that he talked. I know I cried for some time after getting off the phone with him. But I have never forgotten the power of hearing someone who had suffered with a fatal disease his entire short life talk about how blessed he had been, and how grateful he was to God for all he had.

Perhaps you have childhood memories like mine, of grownups trying to get you to eat what was on your plate because there were starving children somewhere else in the world. The basic message was that we were to be grateful for what we had in comparison to others. While that is certainly true, Bill's farewell conversation taught me that comparing myself to others in order to feel gratitude is not terribly helpful. From my perspective, Bill had many reasons to be far less than pleased with the kind of life he had inherited, but he saw it differently. He had argued with God and finally made peace with his disease, and when he did so, he discovered a loving God, rather than a vengeful one, and Bill's response to that was gratitude.

Thankfulness is not something that can be faked very successfully. I was not particularly grateful for the brussel sprouts on my plate when I was six, even though I had them and a child in India did not. Still, we can begin to practice the discipline of noticing people and things for which we are truly grateful. When I made a major move across the country some years ago I was often overwhelmed with feelings of loneliness and homesickness. So I developed the practice of taking a few moments each evening to recall people or events of that day that I was thankful for, even if that was just for my much coveted first cup of coffee that morning. I didn't make anything up, and didn't offer thanks for things I wasn't grateful for. It was hard to do at first, and it didn't decrease my sadness right away. My sadness was the stronger emotion and commanded more of my attention than joy did. But over time it helped me shift my focus to the gifts of my new life, instead of the losses from my old one.

Most of us have more blessings than we count on a given day. These can include the places we live, the people we know, our jobs, a favorite nightshirt, a pet, vanilla ice cream covered with hot fudge on a cold winter's night, and a thousand other joys in our lives. It is so much easier, however, to focus on what is wrong than on what we have to be grateful for, and it takes effort to refocus ourselves. The monks who followed The Rule of the Master, quoted above, made meals one of the things for which they expressed gratitude. The whole community began and ended the meal with the phrase "Thanks be to God," plus other prayers. The rule even tells us that a pulley system delivered the first basket of bread to the abbot immediately after the prayers, "to give the impression that the provisions of God's workmen are coming down from heaven."9 What a sight that must have been! Perhaps we would all be better off if we had such a visible daily reminder of where our gifts in life actually come from.

Practice

Commit yourself to noticing your blessings, and saying thank you to God and to others for them. Try some of the following suggestions or add your own:

1. Take the time to write thank-you notes in response to gifts you've received, events you've enjoyed, or anything else that deserves thanks.

2. Say thank you to other people as often as possible.

3. Say grace before and after meals in thankfulness for the food that sustains your body.

4. Give God a quick thank you throughout the day for anything that gives you joy.

5. Take a daily inventory of the blessings of that particular day. If you wish, keep a written list of these and see if it grows longer over time.

Seek the Will of God

"By these words He [Jesus] teaches us always to place before ourselves as a goal, in undertaking a task, the will of Him who has enjoined the work, and to direct our effort toward Him . . ."

—The Long Rules of St. Basil

A few years ago I was asked to consider a job that I didn't think I wanted. I spent a couple months contemplating the offer, made lists of pros and cons, prayed, and concluded that the job was not for me. I had a lot of good reasons for not taking the job, including a move across the country that I didn't particularly want to make. Those who wanted to hire me felt otherwise, however, and finally convinced me to come for an interview. I was very clear going into the interview that I wasn't going to take the job and had told everyone so. I had bought opera tickets with friends for the upcoming season where I lived, informed all my friends that I wasn't moving, and made many plans for the upcoming year. But God had other plans for me. In the middle of the two days of interviewing with the prospective company I got hit with a sense of call that was so strong that I knew I would be moving and starting a whole new life. God let me fumble around for a few months thinking things through logically, but in the end I threw logic out the window and went where I felt God called me to be.

I say "where I felt God called me" deliberately, because none of us can ever claim with total certainty that we know God's will. And rarely in my life has my sense of God's call been as obvious to me as the story above might imply. There are no easy ways to know if we are following the will of God instead of our own desires. Angels do not generally come down from heaven and give us a thumbs-up when we make the right choice. Flashing lights and buzzers do not go off when we pick correctly, like they do with contestants on game shows. Nor can we always trust our gut instincts that frequently offer us good guidance. Even with the best of intentions we will sometimes do our own will and what pleases us, rather than what might please God more.

Perhaps that is behind the recent fad of items with the initials WWJD on them. WWJD stands for *What Would Jesus Do?* and contemplating that is part of what helps us discern God's will. We can think about what response Jesus— or someone else whose life we admire—might make to a given situation in our life. Confronted with racism, for instance, we might consider what kind of response Martin Luther King, Jr., would ask of us.

Paying attention to our desires in understanding God's will is also important, though tricky. One school of thought suggests that we distrust any and all of our desires implicitly, recognizing that we all too easily fool ourselves into believing that what we want must be what God wants for us. The other school of thought believes that we must listen to our desires, for God may be speaking to us through them. A careful balance of both of these views, however, may help us with seeking God's will. If a desire remains with us over a period of time and through a variety of circumstances, and is not just a passing whim or an impulsive response to something, that desire may actually be the way God is speaking to us. We can also test those desires by asking if what we plan to do helps to bring about some greater good or contributes to the welfare of others. Without over- or underestimating our gifts and skills, does what we feel called to do or be bring benefits to others besides ourselves? If it does, perhaps this is what God calls us to right now. Another helpful strategy for finding our way through the thicket of our own will versus God's is to talk through our perceptions with someone else. A trusted clergyperson or spiritual director are ideal choices for such conversations, but any friend you trust to tell you the truth can be helpful. Friends and spiritual advisors can often help us recognize when we are deceiving ourselves by following only our own desires versus God's call to us.

Practice

1. Form the habit of considering what God would ask you to do in any given situation. As you interact with others or make decisions, make a conscious effort to ask yourself how God would respond in the same situation. Some people will be able to do that spontaneously as the day progresses. Another strategy, particularly for those with busy days, is to take a few moments in the morning before things get rolling to look ahead to the events that you know will take place. By thinking about what God might ask of you in a given situation or by praying for guid-

ance when you need it, you may be more able to discern how God would have you act when the time comes.

2. Review the day during the evening, and make note of the times when you felt you were responding as God would versus the times when you responded in a way that met only your own needs. This may also help you to be more conscious of the process of seeking God's will in your life.

Contemplate God Everywhere

"Learn, too, to contemplate the beauty and holiness of the city where God resides and where he has placed you. There, at the heart of the city, raise your arms in praise and intercession."

—The Jerusalem Community Rule of Life

Close your mind and imagine a deeply holy space. If you're like most of us, specific images will probably come to mind: majestic mountains, stark deserts, the sea, quiet and dark woods. Around you are probably beautiful flowers, birds, calm lakes, stars, or moonlight. Sounds like the ocean roaring and birds singing or even the sound of silence may supplement your picture, while you imagine the smells of flowers, pine trees, saltwater, or sand. Now plop yourself down in the middle of New York City, Washington, D.C., at rush hour, or even your own town, and imagine that as holy space. It is pretty difficult to imagine meditating in the middle of Times Square, Trafalgar Square, or any number of other busy and noisy spots, and truthfully, closing your eyes and sitting down and meditating in those situations is probably not particularly safe. Still, we tend to limit our experience of the holy to places of nature, forgetting that God also lives in the city, in the midst of rush hour traffic, and in the people we brush by without noticing. By recognizing God's presence only in particular environments, and by forgetting God's presence in the workplace, the streets, the movie theater, the grocery store, or wherever we go, we limit our own experience of the sacred and cut ourselves and others off from the presence of God as it flows through us all day long.

Your spiritual life need not be limited to times of prayer, meditation, or worship. It is portable and exists with you every moment of the day. You cannot leave it behind any more than you can leave God behind; you can only choose to remain unconscious of the presence of what is holy. By remaining in touch with God as often as possible, however, you can find opportunities to witness the power of God's love for everything and everyone around you. A friend of mine tells about being on a city bus one day where a young man, apparently agitated, was being loud and abusive to others on the bus. She did not feel physically capable of intervening, but she is a strong woman of prayer. So she imagined him wrapped in God's calming love and the young man did relax and stop yelling at others. I do not believe that our prayers are magic or that they work to our specifications, but I do believe that in this situation her will and God's coincided and that her prayers were part of the man's calming down. We can all bring the power of our own prayers into many situations—youthful violence, short tempers, poverty—that need healing, and be witnesses to the power of God's love.

Perhaps it is easier for most of us to tap into God's presence in particular environments that we have dubbed sacred, but a little willingness to discover the sacred everywhere and some practice is all that is required for deepening our connection to God in all places. Communities, cities, and being in the midst of everything presents us with unique spiritual opportunities often lacking in solitary environments. St. Basil, in the fourth century, founded monasteries partly in opposition to the spiritual hermits of the time, who lived harsh and ascetic lives in the desert. Basil concluded that the solitary search for God led to prideful behavior and provided no opportunity to learn humility or patience or to practice care of others. It did not allow those seeking God to fulfill one of the greatest Christian commandments, which is to love one's neighbor as oneself. ". . . [T]he solitary life removed from all others has only one aim, that of serving the ends of the individual concerned. But this is manifestly opposed to the law of charity . . . We have been called in one hope of our calling, are one body, and members of one another."[10]

The concern that private devotions and our own personal search for God will take us away from the actual presence of God in and around us all the time is no less real today than in was in the fourth century. None of the great spiritual masters, including St. Basil, would prevent us from going off into quiet, natural spaces for meditation of God; all would, in fact, encourage that. But they also call us back to the cities, where many monasteries have been located, in order to pay attention to God's presence in those around us, and to be the presence of God to others. There, in the midst of everything, the Jerusalem Community Rule reminds us, we can raise our arms in praise and intercession—praise for the actual beauty of the city and its many rich resources, and intercession for those who live in poverty in our inner cities or who wander the streets without a place to sleep.

Practice

1. Recognizing the sacred in the midst of the city or wherever you happen to be is mostly a matter of practicing paying attention. "Learn to contemplate the beauty and holiness . . ." the Jerusalem Community Rule suggests. Take a walk somewhere in the city or town in which you live and look specifically for beauty and holiness. Go ahead and notice trees, flowers, birds, and other things we often associate with beauty, but look, too, for signs of beauty and holiness in the buildings around you, the storefront displays, the decorations people have used, the materials from which things are made, and whatever else comes to mind. Pay attention, as well, to the people you encounter.

2. What evidence do you see that God lives within all the people you come across? Can you find beauty and holiness in their faces or action?

3. Finally, notice in what ways you contribute, or can contribute, to bringing the presence of God onto the city streets. Does your appreciation of what you see add anything to the day of another person? Does an offer of assistance help a neighbor in need? How does your own presence in this environment speak of God's presence in the midst of the city?

CHAPTER FOUR

Prayer

"Pray temperately and simply. Prayer is a heart-to-heart talk between yourself and God and needs no brilliant ideas, no flood of words."
—The Jerusalem Community Rule of Life

While some monastic rules fail to address the needs of the body or the earth, all rules include commitments to prayer. It is the basic building block of our relationship with God. Like the visits we make to a sick friend or the phone call congratulating someone or commiserating with them, prayer is essential to being in a relationship with God.

Prayer serves many different functions. It is the time we set aside simply to be with God, just as we make time to be with friends, families, and loved ones. We make time to spend with God, as with others about whom we care, in part because we are beloved and that feels good, and in part because we want to respond to the love we have been given. Prayer is both a gift and a response to that gift.

The time we spend in prayer deepens our relationship with God. It does not always feel natural at first. Sometimes we don't know what to say in the beginning or we spend our time trying to impress God instead of just being ourselves. We talk too much and fail to listen enough or we just don't set aside the quality time to give to the relationship in the first place. But over time a regular prayer life builds a strong relationship, and that practice can sustain us when difficult things happen in our lives. A strong bond with God developed through the practice of prayer will not prevent bad things from happening to us, but it may help us weather the tough days with a little more confidence.

Prayer is also a time for hearing the truth. Sometimes the things we learn in prayer are affirming—we are reminded of our great value and of God's unconditional love for us. Other times we hear truths that are harder to accept. Perhaps we know we have been engaged in something that is not good for us or which is unhealthy or dangerous for someone else. Or maybe we begin to understand that the path we are on is not one that God calls us to follow. Often, I find myself avoiding prayer at times when I am not sure that I want to hear the truth, when I want to do what I'm doing regardless of the consequences, or when I'm feeling resistant to change. Prayer, if we are being attentive, is a time of listening and discernment, of guidance and affirmation. We may not always hear what we hope to hear.

Still, prayer times are opportunities to tell God what is on our minds and hearts. It is not that God is unaware of those joys and sorrows that we carry with us. Those who are close to us often know what is pleasing or troubling us, sometimes before we do, and God is no exception. But our need to tell the stories of our life is always strong. It is often in the telling that we come to understand the fullness of our own experiences.

There are as many ways, places, and times to pray as there

are individuals in this world, and literally hundreds of books about the practice of prayer are published every year. The following practices, however, are some basic ones you might incorporate into a rule of life. You may wish to choose only one that makes the most sense to you or choose a group of them in combination. You could, for instance, have one prayer practice for very busy days when you have little free time and another discipline for those days during which you can pray for a long period. If you are not familiar with the practices, experiment with some of them and see which ones speak to you most clearly.

Set Aside a Place for Prayer

"The place of prayer should not be used for any purpose other than that for which it is intended and from which it takes its name."

—The Rule of St. Augustine

Have you ever had the experience of wandering into a sanctuary or a chapel and felt yourself surrounded by the prayers of thousands who have been in this space before you? In such a place there is a sense of the hopes, dreams, the angst and pain of countless people who have prayed within its walls. The presence of the prayers is palpable and it draws you—almost pulls you—into prayer yourself. These spaces reserved for the prayers of the people of God are instantly recognizable as sacred and they speak deeply and directly to the soul. We pray almost without knowing that we are doing so.

We do not need to go to a church, however, in order to have that experience. Just as monks and nuns have a chapel located within the monastery in which they live, we, too, can create a prayer corner or altar in our home that becomes sacred prayer space for us. If we pray in it often, it begins to fill with the sense of our prayers and becomes more and more holy to us. Our bodies begin to recognize the space when we enter it, and prayer comes more easily there than it does in other places.

My own favorite prayer corner was in a spare room of a house I lived in once. The room was sunny and airy and I placed an old, ratty, and very comfortable stuffed chair facing a window that looked out over lots of trees and flowers. On a table next to the chair were my favorite prayer books, my rosary, a couple of icons, a candle, and some rocks that I've picked up on retreats over the years. On a bookshelf on the other side of the chair was a statue of a person kneeling in front of Jesus, who lays his healing hands on the person's head. When I first began to use the prayer corner it felt the same as praying in any other space of my house. There was no sense that this place was any more holy than any other in my home. Over time, however, the prayer corner became sacred for me. When I sat there, my body remembered the chair and the place and knew that I was there to pray. I could settle into deep prayer there with very little effort.

Over time the use of a prayer corner or room tends to deepen our prayer lives. The body has a memory of its own, and as you spend more time in the space, you will probably experience yourself being pulled into prayer even upon entering it. Though God is with me always, I am most aware of God's presence in my prayer corner. Sensing God there with me, prayer—my conversation with God—pours forth.

Practice

A prayer corner, altar, or a room set aside for prayer can be as simple or elaborate as you choose. If having this kind of area would enhance your prayer time, try the following simple steps. These suggestions assume an ideal situation for setting up a prayer room or corner. You may need to make some compromises depending on the space you have available, your family situation, or other factors.

1. Walk around your home quietly and attentively, noting your feelings and responses to particular rooms or portions of rooms. If there is a particular space that you are drawn to for any reason, perhaps it would make a good prayer place for you. If nothing presents itself to you as the ideal area, select a spot in which you would like to spend some time.

2. Make the space a private one if you are able, someplace where you can close yourself off from family members, roommates, or other people.

3. Provided it is possible, dedicate this space to prayer alone.

4. Clear the space of distractions if you can. Remove telephones, fax machines, pagers, loud clocks, or anything else that would disturb your prayers.

5. Some of the furniture and objects you might consider in your prayer corner are:

   • Something comfortable on which to sit: a chair, couch, mat, or pillow that supports your body and does not cut off circulation

   • A prayer stool or kneeler

   • Stereo, CD or tape player

   • Incense burner

- Icons

- Candles

- Devotional or prayer books, the Bible

- Prayer beads or rosary

- Religious artwork or artwork that helps you pray

- Bells or other objects that might open and close your prayer time

- Flowers or other natural objects

- A journal

- Any object that helps you pray

6. The first time you pray in your new prayer corner, take a few moments to invite God into this space most particularly. Just as you might spend time with a good friend in a favorite coffee shop, restaurant, or on a park bench, this space is one in which you will spend time with God. Take a little time getting to know your space and invite God to participate in making it holy ground.

7. Pray regularly in this space. Only repeated use will fill it with your prayers and make it holy ground.

Practice Silence

"Interior silence requires first of all to forget oneself, to quiet discordant voices, and to master obsessing worry . . . Interior silence renders possible our conversation with Jesus Christ."

—The Rule of Taizé

One of the most important, and often the most difficult, parts of prayer is learning to be silent and listen to God. Continuing the analogy of prayer as a conversation with a close friend, think about how difficult a one-sided relationship is. When one person does all the talking and fails to listen well it is extremely difficult for a meaningful relationship to develop.

Silence, however, is harder to maintain than a balanced conversation. Turning off all the chatter in our minds—what some Eastern traditions have called Monkey Mind—is very difficult. If you don't believe me, stop for a moment and try it. Just close your eyes and try to be perfectly still for even thirty seconds without your attention drifting off. Unless you have had some training in this area, chances are you noticed several thoughts crossing your mind in those thirty seconds. The world we live in does not encourage or reward silence. Many of us live in noisy cities and we hardly notice the conversations occurring around us, the blare of cars, radios, televisions, or even the hum of machinery around us. (It wasn't until I typed that last sentence that I began to hear the noise my computer makes.) We are accustomed to noise in our world. Silence is something we think of with a certain amount of anxiety; the ultimate silence is that of the grave. We do not necessarily welcome or court silence in our world.

Nonetheless, it is very hard to hear God guiding us when we are afraid of silence and incapable of being still once in a while. As a friend of mine wrote, somewhat humorously: "Pray, certainly. But stop your mouth and listen, too. God is usually very polite, and loathe to interrupt."[11] Learning to be silent is no different than developing strong muscles; it takes practice. As with exercise, if you are not accustomed to silence you may also be uncomfortable as you begin learning how to quiet yourself. You will probably feel the urge to do anything but sit quietly and listen for God as you begin and that is perfectly natural. Be gentle with yourself at first and do not ask too much of yourself. Anyone who has not exercised in years and begins with a two-hour workout with heavy weights will likely be miserable and give up exercising. So, too, with the discipline of silence. Using some of the suggestions below, begin with short sessions—even just a couple of minutes—and gradually work your way up to longer sessions of fifteen minutes or more. You might even try practicing silence with a prayer partner or a prayer group if you have one. Sometimes the companionship and the desire to avoid disturbing someone else's silence can help you stay with the discomfort you feel. The presence of another person or a group in silence can also bring about something of the same sense that a prayer corner does—the room fills with the silence and listening of all involved and God's presence is sometimes more easily felt in this environment.

Practice

There are a variety of different methods you can use to help quiet the chatter in your mind. In all of the following you will probably notice various thoughts about your day, concerns, or things to be done floating into your consciousness. Gently dismiss them without judging them or yourself and return to the practice you've selected. Or write down your distracting thoughts and concerns and make a deal with yourself that you will return to them later. The first two practices are useful for individuals or groups, while the third is for individual use only.

1. Sit in a comfortable position, close your eyes, and focus on your breathing. Breathe fully without exaggerating the movement and try to concentrate on noticing your breaths in and out. Imagine that you are breathing in the grace and love of God and breathing out all of your concerns, frustrations, or worries.

2. Sit in a comfortable position with your eyes open. Focus your attention on a devotional object of your choice—a candle, icon, something in nature, or whatever reminds you of God's presence. Use the object as a focus, clearing your mind of other thoughts. Let the object speak to you of God.

3. Walking can be a very meditative activity, and can be particularly useful when combined with a short prayer. Try to find a place to walk that is not crowded, where you will not have to concentrate on avoiding others. With a one-line or short prayer of your choice, walk along, repeating the prayer in time with your steps. With practice the prayer will become almost automatic and even though you are praying you will also find your mind is silent and clear.

Pray Without Ceasing

"Resisting the tendency to restrict prayer to set times, we are to aim at eucharistic living that is responsive at all times and in all places to the divine presence. We should seek the gifts which help us to pray without ceasing."
—The Rule of the Society of St. John the Evangelist

I can almost see you staring at me in incredulity when I suggest to you that you pray without ceasing. That might be a good suggestion for a hermit who has nothing else to do in this world, but you probably need to earn a living and maintain a household of some sort. And in all likelihood, living the life of a hermit has little appeal to you except, perhaps, on really bad days.

But praying without ceasing does not mean that we sit cross-legged praying a mantra twenty-four hours a day, seven days a week. We pray without ceasing when we try to remain conscious of God's presence throughout the day by constantly returning our focus to God. In monasteries and convents this is done, in part, by observing regularly scheduled periods of prayer, known as praying the hours. All through the day and even well into the night in some places, monks or nuns gather to pray services established for that particular time of day or evening. The practice allows the participant's focus to return regularly to God.

Most of us, however, will find it difficult to stop and pray the hours as they are done in an enclosed environment, but it is still possible to deliberately focus on God's presence in our daily lives. *The Rule of the Society of St. John the Evangelist* suggests that the gifts that help us pray without ceasing include: attentiveness to God's presence and actions; the cessation of anxiety and fearfulness that prevent us from being present to God; the practice of spontaneous prayers throughout the day; and asking for forgiveness promptly when we do something wrong.[12] In other words, we pray without ceasing when we consciously seek God in everything and everyone who surrounds us, and respond to them as we would respond to God. When we stop for a moment to give thanks or to ask for help or forgiveness, even just for thirty seconds, we are praying. The more often we do that, and the more often we stop to notice God's presence during the day or night, the closer we come to praying without ceasing. Brother Lawrence, a fifteenth-century monk, is an excellent guide to this kind of prayer. His concise book, *The Practice of the Presence of God*, available in many editions and translations, has helped many generations learn to seek and acknowledge the presence of God in everything they do and in everyone they encounter daily.

I remember discovering this kind of prayer several years ago. Without thinking about it one day, I stopped for a few seconds and thanked God for something that had just happened. It wasn't a conscious decision to pray on my part, simply a spontaneous response to a wonderful event, and I realized that this was just as much prayer as the longer periods of time I'd previously felt were required for praying. On days when I didn't have ten minutes or a half hour to set aside as prayer time, and even on the days when I did, I began to simply notice the things for which I was thankful, the events or people that worried me, the things I did that I was sorry for. I stopped when I noticed God's presence in one of these ways, and in the time it took me to breathe deeply once or twice, I spoke a quick, one-sentence prayer to God. In doing that, I became far more aware of God's presence in my daily life rather than simply during my prayer times. I was learning to pray without ceasing.

Practice

To learn to pray without ceasing use your daily activities as a springboard for prayer. (This is a strategy used by the Celts in early Christian history. They had blessings for rising, lighting the fire, and many of their other daily activities.)

1. Begin by making a list of the things you do in a given day: rising from bed, taking a shower, eating, and so on. You can use all of these as opportunities for a spontaneous prayer of your own or a prayer that you have selected to fit each activity. Those prayers can be ones you've composed or they can come from a prayer book, a collection of sacred poetry, or other books you find prayerful. The Bible, and particularly the Psalms, is a wonderful place to find simple one-line prayers. The following are suggestions from the Bible that you might find helpful in daily prayer.

- Upon waking up in the morning: "This is the day the Lord has made; let us rejoice and be glad in it." (Psalm 118:24)

- During your shower: "Create in me a clean heart, O God, and put a new and right spirit within me." (Psalm 51:10)

- Getting dressed: "O Lord my God, you are very great. You are clothed with honor and majesty, wrapped in light as with a garment." (Psalm 104:1–2)

- Commuting: "Make me to know your ways, O Lord; teach me your paths." (Psalm 25:4)

- Beginning the day's work: "Let the favor of the Lord our God be upon us, and prosper for us the work of our hands." (Psalm 90:17)

- Thankfulness for something good: "Blessed be the Lord, the God of Israel, who alone does wondrous things." (Psalm 72:18)

- During a difficult day: "I lift up my eyes to the hills—from where will my help come? My help comes from the Lord, who made heaven and earth." (Psalm 121:1–2)

- When you regret doing something: "For your name's sake, O Lord, pardon my guilt, for it is great." (Psalm 25:11)

- At the end of work: "All your works praise you, O Lord, and your faithful servants bless you." (Psalm 145:10)

- At meals: "I am the living bread that came down from heaven. Whoever eats of this bread will live forever; and the bread that I will give for the life of the world is my flesh." (John 6:51)

- At bedtime: "I bless the Lord who gives me counsel; in the night also my heart instructs me." (Psalm 16:7)

2. Learning to become aware of God's presence continually, like any other discipline, requires some practice. We get caught up in the activities of the day very easily and our focus shifts away from God repeatedly. Try to avoid criticizing yourself for not being able to master praying without ceasing instantly; give yourself ample time to develop this practice. Figure skaters, after all, do not learn to do a triple jump in a day and you will not learn to pray without ceasing instantly. Even Brother Lawrence, admired for his ability to see God in everything and everyone, found this difficult, but he offers us words of encouragement: "[I]n the beginning a persistent effort is needed to form the habit of continually talking with God and to refer all we do to Him but . . . after a little care His love brings us to it without any difficulty."[13]

Pray for Your Enemies

"Pray constantly for those who annoy you."
—The Rule of Colmcille

Perhaps you struggle, as I do, with feelings of resentment and annoyance. There are the day-to-day petty irritations, like having a driver cut you off on the road. Then there are the major grudges that we harbor, the ones that don't go away easily. In my own life, there was someone who once did great harm to me emotionally. From today's vantage point, I can say that she did not do this with malice toward me specifically—she just didn't know any other way to respond. For many years after I extricated myself from the situation and was free from her influence in my life I retained and nurtured my anger toward her with all my strength. The hatred became my excuse for everything, a cornerstone of my existence. It even had its positive uses and fueled some of the successes of my life. At least a decade passed before I realized how destructive that anger was to my own soul. Even though we were separated by great distances it was as if some invisible pipeline connected us and fed the resentments. It was only after I began to understand how harmful this was to me as well as to her that I began to dismantle the pipeline and let go of the hatred. I began to pray for the well-being of the one who had harmed me, and in time the prayers were from the heart instead of a sense of propriety.

It is easy to despise ourselves for hating others and there is no question that hatred is harmful. But I take some solace in the fact that even the Bible is filled with mean-spirited behavior—that I am not the first or only person in the world to struggle with this problem. Take, for instance, the story of God drowning all the Egyptians in the sea, after having parted the waters to let Moses and the Israelites escape. The Psalms, too, are full of references to our enemies or those who are generally wicked. The beautiful Psalm 139 abruptly turns harsh at verse 19: "Oh that you would kill the wicked, O God, and that the bloodthirsty would depart from me." Psalm 143 speaks from the same perspective: "For your name's sake, O Lord, preserve my life. In your righteousness bring me out of trouble. In your steadfast love cut off my enemies, and destroy all my adversaries. For I am your servant." (Psalm 143:11–12) Psalm 137 even portrays satisfaction in dashing the enemy's little children against rocks. Most of us recoil at the self-righteous tone and sheer violence of these kinds of passages, and with good reason. But when we are honest with ourselves we must also admit that each of us has the capacity for this level of hatred, that we have these same kinds of thoughts from time to time.

Perhaps, then, it is just as well that we find these emotions spoken in the Bible as reminders of our own darker side. We must acknowledge these feelings and be aware that even Jesus got very angry; we cannot expect ourselves to be happy and kind at all times. The problem with holding on to these angers and vendettas, however, is the harm they do not only to those who annoy us, but to ourselves. If we put forth anger, hatred, and vengeance on a regular basis we work against God's will for the world and help to tie God's hands, metaphorically speaking. When we wish each other well we provide material and nourishment for God's hopes for our world and we participate in bringing about peace on earth. Thus we can choose to help God in making the world a gentler place or we can make one that is increasingly violent and dangerous.

Praying for others, however, also affects our own thoughts and feelings, as much as or perhaps more than it influences others. Over time, praying for those who annoy us teaches us compassion and brings about change in our own hearts. Praying for those who irritate us may also provide us with clues about our own problems; it is not unusual to dislike a quality in another person that we find annoying in ourselves. Praying for others can help us to see our "enemies" in a different light and help us to forgive someone who has harmed us, not for their sake, but so we can move on with our own lives.

The hatreds we harbor separate us from God. God does not love us any less when our hearts are full of anger and vengeance, but in this state it is very difficult for us to claim God's love fully. Praying for those who annoy us can help to restore within us the compassion that God asks us to spread in the world, on God's behalf. It brings us back into right relationship with others and with God.

Practice

While you may have a list of people who annoy you and you may want to pray for all of them, it can be most helpful to focus intensely on one person at a time, to really put some effort, thought, and prayer into a particular relationship. Focusing on everyone at once will often prevent you from spending the energy and thought required to truly heal a grudge you are carrying.

1. Think of someone who annoys you, against whom you harbor some resentment. Ask yourself if you are willing to pray for this person, even if you do not yet wish him or her well.

2. If you are willing to pray for this person, begin with a very simple prayer. It needs to be an honest expression of your feelings, something as basic as: "Dear God, I feel nothing but anger against X, but I would like to feel differently. Please surround us both with your love and grace at this difficult time." Pray your own thoughts, whatever they are, knowing that God is already aware of your feelings. Be sure to include a positive prayer for the other person as well. Give God something to work with in healing the damage done in your particular situation.

3. Commit to holding this person and your own needs in the situation in prayer regularly—daily if you can. As the weeks pass see if the act of praying for the one who annoys you helps you to see the relationship differently and if it affects how you relate to God. Is there any sense of your heart softening over time? Does forgiveness seem possible, even if reconciliation is impossible? Does your gradual release of the hatred or annoyance allow you to move closer to God?

4. Continue to hold this person, and any others who annoy you, in prayer for as long as it is necessary. Be gentle with yourself if a change of your own heart does not occur immediately. Prayer is not magic and does not "work" overnight. But if you continue the practice in good faith, in time your heart will soften.

Pray Many Ways

"Your prayer will take countless forms because it is the echo of your life, and a reflection of the inexhaustible light in which God dwells."

—Rule for a New Brother

In my experience, most people, when they visualize prayer as an activity, think of one of two things—Sunday morning prayer in church and private prayer. They most often think of prayer as something quiet and contemplative. The increased awareness of Eastern faiths and meditative practices in the last couple of decades has helped Christians and Jews to revive their own contemplative traditions, and it is this influence we see in small prayer groups, retreats, and private devotions today. These practices suit many people well, particularly those whose spirituality is introverted and who need time alone in order to get rejuvenated. It is not, however, the whole picture. Prayer, as the Rule for a New Brother states, "takes countless forms," and before we berate ourselves for not praying formally each and every day, perhaps it is helpful to recognize the other ways in which we pray.

If prayer is communicating with and listening for God in our lives, any activity that helps us connect with God can become prayer. In other words, anything that helps us express our concerns, share our frustrations, offer our confessions and thanksgivings, and listen for guidance, can be prayer. A friend of mine who is a New Testament scholar says that he does not attend church anymore, but that his study of the Bible is prayer for him. Reading and studying the biblical texts has become his way of communicating with God and listening for God's guidance in his life. Another friend experiences communion with God through dance and improvisation. Letting go of his own inhibitions and relying on God to give him the movements and interpretations he needs allows him to be close to God, to rest in God's presence. For him, movement and play are prayer. Yet another acquaintance of mine is energized by being around people. She feels God's presence when she talks with others. God and prayer live, for her, in caring and thoughtful conversation with the people in her world.

For me, writing is praying. I find that often when I am not writing, the time I spend in formal prayer is dry and lifeless. I am one of those people who finds God in quiet, contemplative prayer and it is a regular part of my life. But I find that this formal prayer time is enriched by the conversations I have with God through my writing. The process of writing demands that I draw on the knowledge of those who came before me, and that I search my own heart and soul for wisdom, and for what God might have me write. My writing time, on the other hand, is enriched by the long walks I take, during which I clear my head of daily annoyances and distractions. When I am stuck in my writing a walk often clarifies my thinking. It is not unusual for whole sections of a chapter to come to me while out walking, without much conscious effort on my part. I consider these gifts from God, something that results from our ongoing conversation. So for me, walking and writing are as much prayer as the formal time I spend in contemplation, Bible reading, or the Evening Prayer service.

Practice

Too often we berate ourselves for not spending some specified period in formal prayer on a daily basis. Regular periods of prayer are certainly important, though the frequency and method will vary from person to person. Instead of feeling guilty for the prayer time you are not taking, perhaps it would be useful to recognize the other ways in which you find connection with God—the other ways in which you pray.

1. Think back over your life and make a list of times when you felt especially close to God or felt God's guidance in your life. Try to remember the details of those events: where you were; what was happening in your life at the time; the feelings you had before, during, and after your experience of God's presence. For instance, I used to feel close to God and very peaceful at a summer music camp I attended. It was out in the woods, by a lake, and I found great tranquillity and joy in sitting in the woods listening to all sorts of people playing their instruments in various buildings and forest glades. I had a bodily sense of great expansiveness and deep relaxation, and an astonishment at the greatness of God's creation. Re-

call your own memories of moments when you felt close to God.

2. What activities in your life leave you feeling spiritually alive? For me, some of those activities are quilting, writing, reading, walking, intimate conversation with a close friend, making love, listening to music. What things do you enjoy doing that seem to be a wake-up call to your soul somehow? Write some of these memories and activities on a list if you wish. Try to refer to this list regularly until you become more aware of these activities as prayer in your life.

3. When you do something that opens you spiritually or you have an experience of God's presence take a moment to dedicate that to God and to ask for guidance, forgiveness, or to offer thanksgiving as appropriate.

Embrace Periods of Dryness in Your Prayer

"There will be days when the office [daily prayer] is a burden to you. On such occasions know how to offer your body, since your presence itself already signifies your desire, momentarily unrealizable, to praise your Lord."

—The Rule of Taizé

It is easy enough for me to pray regularly when prayer is accompanied by feelings of peacefulness, relaxation, or a sense of God's presence around me. Prayer on those days is like a deep and satisfying conversation. There are other days, however, when it feels like "nothing happens" when I pray. Some days I am too stressed or tired to be attentive to God's presence or God just seems to be absent. Even when everything is going well in my life and my prayer time, sometimes suddenly the well of prayer is "dry" for no apparent reason. God is not exactly absent, but I am not deeply aware of

God's presence either. Both of these situations can lead to frustration, irritation, and self-doubt. Who are we, after all, to think that God is interested in our measly little prayer life?

Our most natural response to periods of dryness in prayer is to just stop praying. If "nothing is happening," then why bother? But what if we approached conversation with a good friend in the same way, breaking off contact with that person when the relationship wasn't stimulating enough for a little while? We would soon be friendless. Every relationship—those with friends as well as with God—goes through periods of intense connection and times when very little seems to be happening. This is normal for most relationships. Much as a real marriage is not about the first rush of infatuation and love, a real relationship with God gets forged by being attentive and present when nothing much is happening. How we live in the ordinary daily times of our life, the little things we do and the connections we make, are the things that truly deepen relationships, even when it seems as if we are not making any particular connection at the moment.

Times of dryness in prayer may also occur when we are completing or beginning a transition in our spiritual life. When I have been focusing very hard on some aspect of my spiritual journey and I finally begin to understand where God is leading me, I often find my prayer life drying up for a while. I use the analogy of mountain climbing to understand these periods: After a long time of struggle and climbing I reach a plateau or some flat ground where my body (or soul) can rest for a while before the next steep incline. When I was younger I used to miss the thrill of the climb—the search for God's direction—when I hit the plateau. These days I am grateful for the rest and more able to embrace these gentle, transitional periods that help me absorb what I have learned. These dry periods can also be precursors to spiritual change, allowing you time to prepare for the journey, to begin asking the questions you need to ask, to motivate you for the next climb.

Dry periods also happen when we are too tired or stressed to be truly present in prayer, no matter how much we wish to be attentive to God. Sometimes this is just a day or a week. Other times we find ourselves in difficult life circumstances and our ability to pray actively is limited. Perhaps we are working too hard for a while or we are dealing with an illness that exhausts us. When I find myself in a place like this I turn to alternate kinds of prayer that require less energy from me, but that help me be aware of God and gather strength from that relationship. One of my best "I'm too tired to pray" prayers is to listen to a tape of sung evening prayer that I love. I can let the words and music wash over me and let the prayers of the musicians and singers be my prayers. This gives me the time I need to focus on God, to be in God's presence, but does not require very much energy on my part.

There are many different reasons why our prayer lives dry up sometimes, but the response to all of them is basically the same. Try to embrace these desert times that have as much to teach us—and perhaps more—as the peak experiences of prayer. Keep praying even if "nothing is happening." Much may be occurring of which you are currently unaware.

Practice

When inevitable periods of dryness occur in prayer, try some of the following:

1. Ask for God's guidance to understand what may be needed during this stage of your spiritual life. Try to be patient and wait while you listen for an answer.

2. Continue to pray in your usual way, confident that something is actually happening, even if you can't sense it at the time. Sometimes dryness in prayer is just familiarity or boredom; by staying with the practice to which you've committed, you may, over time, find it deepening and feeding you in new ways.

3. Ask others to pray for you. Sometimes, particularly when we are ill or at the end of our rope, we need others to offer prayers for us and on our behalf. My spiritual director often prays at the end of our time together. She frequently asks me what I need from God in the coming weeks and asks God for that as she prays. Tell others what you are feeling and need from God and let them help you pray for and with you.

4. There are times when we are just too exhausted to pray and this results in dryness in prayer. Pray some other way for a period of time; listen to music, do something artistic, read something that focuses you on God, such as the spiritual classics, or do some other activity that allows you to pray without expending more energy than you have available to you at the time.

5. Try to relax into the period of dryness, knowing that it has something to teach you or that it is preparation for something in the future. Try to be patient and gentle with yourself and listen for God's guidance during this time.

Make Time for Retreats

"There are moments when the silence of God culminates in his creatures. In the solitude of a retreat, we are renewed by intimate meeting with Christ. These essential moments must therefore be set aside."

—The Rule of Taizé

Not too long ago I had the opportunity to go to London for a week of meetings with my British colleagues. It was my first trip to London and I found myself a bit overwhelmed by the busy, noisy, crowded, fast-paced city. I have very little sense of direction and finding my way on London's curving streets confused and annoyed me. The complexities of the transportation systems and just trying to find the resources I needed in an unfamiliar place exhausted me completely by the week's end. I wanted nothing more than to get on an airplane and go home by Friday. I had left lots of work on my desk before my journey abroad and I knew that much more had come in while I was away. The stresses of getting ready for the trip, being in London, and all the work awaiting me felt oppressive. I just wanted to get back home and try to work my way through my long to-do list in the hope that this would someday reduce the stress I was feeling.

I had been heavily stressed for some months, however, London only exacerbated the feelings. So when I had scheduled the London trip, I also made a space for some retreat time in western Wales. In my bag was a train ticket and bed-and-breakfast reservations, all prepaid, for several days in St. Davids, an ancient pilgrimage site located on the coast of Wales. For months before this trip I had been feeling strained and exhausted. I was working too hard, while resting and playing too little. My spiritual life felt a bit lifeless and more like something on my to-do list than a cornerstone of my existence. So I had scheduled this time-out, a few days of rest and prayer, in a place that was reputed to be quite beautiful. At the end of my week in London, however, I cared very little about all of that and seriously considered chucking the whole thing and just going home.

Perhaps you, like me, find it difficult to put aside time for retreats. After all (I convince myself) being in touch with God every day is far more important and nourishing than putting aside a chunk of time for silence, prayer, and relaxation. The everyday relationship with God is, of course, essential, and we would be lost without it. But the occasional times when we talk deeply and at length with God are powerful building blocks of a meaningful relationship. We don't look for those kinds of conversations on a constant basis; they require too much energy and intensity from us. Still, the times when we engage in these intimate conversations are memorable and important. Our daily prayers and activities need the support of these extended conversations from time to time, and we must make a space for them to happen.

Making space is what retreat is all about. When we are

filled with the demands of daily life, when things gets frantic, sometimes there is very little space for God. There is no opening in the chatter of our minds where God can enter. It is when our own worries, anxieties, and to-do lists fill our lives, when we can hear little besides our own voices, that we most need to make space for retreat time. (Though nothing prevents us from taking time for a retreat even when we are not stressed.)

The space we make can take a variety of shapes. Some people will find that contact with God is best renewed in short, frequent retreats—a morning set aside once a month or some similar schedule. Others find that spending long periods of time—several days or a week or more—less often most helpful. People will also vary in their needs for companionship; some need retreats with others who are seeking God, while others need time alone to pursue their conversations with God. In any of these cases, however, it is usually helpful to retreat someplace away from your normal activities, someplace free of distractions that divert your attention from God. Take as little as possible with you on retreat and take only those things that further your prayer time—a Bible or other sacred reading, a notebook or journal to record your thoughts, perhaps some art materials, candles, or other things that help you focus on your relationship with God. Make an effort to leave daily activities, work, and other concerns behind when you go on retreat. This is a time for you to give God all of your attention and allow that relationship to deepen and grow. Try, also, to go without expectations about what will occur and let God be your guide during this time. Don't be afraid to pray for any needs or worries you have or to offer praise or thanksgiving to God; this isn't a one-way conversation. But try to be open to whatever direction your retreat time takes without needing to be in control. I have yet to go on a retreat where I could have predicted the direction of the conversation or guidance.

That was certainly true of my retreat time in Wales. I did finally drag myself from London to St. Davids, knowing that my frustration with London was probably just one more sign that I was off-balance spiritually, emotionally, and physically. For three days I wandered the cliffs along the coastline. I sat quietly in St. Davids Cathedral for many hours, praying and listening. I visited the ruins of St. Non's Chapel and the holy healing well there, and washed my hands and face in it several times, praying for my heart to reopen to God's presence in my life. And at the end of my time in Wales I felt restored again. After all the restlessness and frustration of the preceding months, I recovered my sense of peacefulness. The hours of prayer and walking taught me some new things about myself, some that I liked and some that I didn't. But on retreat I relocated my center—God—and with that I was able to go back into the world and begin again.

Practice

Set a regular retreat schedule for yourself based on your own needs. Perhaps you can put aside one day a month, or even a morning monthly, to be quiet and listen to God's presence in your life. If you can afford it, and can take the time, try to find a retreat center or a place to go that removes you from your normal environment and all the distractions of phones, people, and the daily tasks you need to do. Use some of the suggested strategies above to slow down and make a holy space for yourself and God.

CHAPTER FIVE

Work

"By choosing to work as hard as possible, but not more than you ought, not primarily in view of a perishable end but one that last for ever, you are to stand free and challenging in a world where work has been overrated into a religion and often into a sacred cow..."
    —The Jerusalem Community Rule of Life

For most of us, work occupies at least eight hours a day, five days a week. A third of most days is spent working and work is an activity that most do not consider a spiritual one. If we don't check God at the door in the morning, at a minimum we marginalize God's place at work. For many of us, however, work has become something like a religion with its own gods and sacred texts. The training for some types of professions—doctors and lawyers, for instance—are initiations into a set of beliefs and practices and seem to be as much an endurance contest as education. Employers today, in an effort to cut back on staff and increase profits, often ask employees who have not been downsized to do the tasks that two people (or more) formerly did. Others are simply addicted to work and find themselves on the job six or seven days a week with no vacation in sight. Work has, indeed, become a sacred cow in today's economy.

Work, however, has always been a major part of our existence, required for our subsistence. Many of the ancient and contemporary rules deal extensively with work, since it is an important part of monastery life. In a community, after all, someone has to cook, clean, grow or shop for food, and care for guests. In the monastery, however, work is never the first priority. It comes after prayer and study and is always balanced with the other activities of the community. Furthermore, work is seen as an extension of prayer and study, not an escape from them. "Your work is no escape into inactivity," says the Rule for a New Brother, "but a sharing in the upbuilding of the body of Christ."[14]

In dealing with work issues, many of the rules reflect the idea that the creation of the world is incomplete, that God continues to strive for a perfect world. Our work, then, can be viewed as a method of continually cocreating the world along with God. Part of our responsibility is to discern what it is that God has for us to do, and then to do it well. We are God's arms, legs, and hands in the world, and our work helps to bring about God's kingdom on earth. "We are called to offer all our work to God," The Rule of the Society of St. John the Evangelist tells us, "and ask for the graces we need to do it in Christ's name."[15] Several of the suggestions in the work chapter will help you to focus on this aspect of work.

If our work is cocreative with God then we must approach the work with holy respect, rather than concentrating exclusively on productivity and efficiency. The people with whom we work and whom we serve, the tools that we use, and the things we produce are all part of God's creation. The decisions that we make about how people will be treated and resources used affect the whole of creation. We are asked to treat these things with dignity, to exercise careful stewardship of all the people and things with which we come into contact. Some suggestions for living these work rules are also included in this chapter.

Finally, we are asked to remember that God is our partner in all that we do, which means that we do not take undue credit for our accomplishments. This also means that we remember to be grateful for the gift of work. A word of caution goes with this, however. A spirituality of the workplace has developed in recent years that is sometimes used as yet another method of boosting productivity. Though looking at work as a spiritual activity may lead to increased efficiency, it is not its goal. We are not called to allow ourselves to overwork or to be humiliated or misused in the workplace in the name of God or spirituality. Many of the suggestions in this chapter encourage you to reexamine your relationships and ways of working in the workplace, to see your work as vocation or calling rather than as a way of earning a living. This is not, however, a call to martyrdom. If you are being treated badly, if you end each day angry and frustrated or without any sense of accomplishment, God may well be calling you to find another job. Spending our days fighting or dealing with people who treat us poorly does not assist God in building a more perfect world.

Abusive situations or bad job fits aside, any work has the potential to be part of building up God's world if we remember to make it so. Part of living a well-balanced life with God at the center of it is learning to recognize God at work with us. Being aware of God at work does not mean evangelizing to others or decorating our work stations with candles, incense, and other items of devotion. Some of us may work in jobs where these activities are appropriate; most of us do not.

Including God in our work means that we remember to consider what God asks of us in a given situation—whether that be kindness to others, the creation of something that assists others, or the prevention of violence or harm or something else—and that we respond to others as we think God would do. The rules in this chapter focus on helping us make God a part of our workday.

Be Grateful for the Gift of Work

"When the day's work is ended, thanksgiving should be offered for what has been granted us or for what we have done rightly therein . . ."

—The Long Rules of St. Basil

F ew of us look at our work as a gift. More of us probably resonate with the passage in Genesis where God curses Adam and Eve for eating the apple. "Cursed is the ground because of you; in toil you shall eat of it all the days of your life . . . By the sweat of your face you shall eat bread until you return to the ground . . ." (Genesis 3:17,19) Most of us feel we work hard for the pay we receive, and finding the gift in our work can be a challenge. Still, we need only look to the unemployed to recognize the value of work. In addition to the deprivation of physical resources such as food, housing, and other necessities, being out of work often robs people of a sense of identity and an important source of satisfaction in life.

In Genesis we read that work was originally given as a

gift. In Genesis 2:15, God "took the man and put him in the garden of Eden to till it and keep it." God gave Adam the freedom to eat anything in the garden but the apples, and provided him with animals and eventually Eve for companionship and help. There is no sense that tilling the garden or naming the animals was loathsome to Adam and Eve; Eden is described as beautiful, filled with rivers and "every tree that is pleasant to the sight and good for food." (Genesis 2:9) Work, then, was originally a gift from God.

A commentary, written to accompany The Rule of the Secular Franciscan Order quoted above, reinforces this theory: "By working, a person shares in the creative power of the Father, renews the face of the earth along with the Son, and brings the love of the Holy Spirit to the human community. Such an attitude toward work can reshape one's own and others' values and actions regarding labor and management, business and economics, living wage and welfare, proper use of one's own talents and the resources of others."[16]

In other words, by focusing on how our work assists God's efforts and on how it helps renew the earth and those around us, we will begin to find the gift in our work. That gift may be in the form of deep satisfaction in the work we turn out or in our recognition of how it serves others. Maybe we are doing work that we feel God called us to do or work that helps build a better earth or society. Unless we are working in a situation that is abusive to our physical, psychological, or spiritual well-being, any job can have within it—directly or indirectly—elements of creativity that serve God's purposes here on earth.

Doing our work well can be an expression of gratitude for what we have been given to do. "Work is not unimportant to God," writes Norvene Vest in her book *Friend of the Soul:*

A Benedictine Spirituality of Work, "but is an expression of gratitude for the gifts we have been given by God and a way to cooperate in God's purposes. Consider your own work in this light for a moment—not so much in terms of what it makes or produces, but rather as one way in which the power of God for transforming good might be introduced into your work setting."[17] In other words, we use the talents God has given us to the best of our ability to help God in transforming the world. In gratitude to God one person teaches kindergarten and another builds houses. Someone else arranges paintings in an art gallery, while another raises his children. We each use the gifts we have to work for the betterment of God's kingdom here on earth.

Practice

Holding our work and our opportunity to serve in esteem means that we use and treat our gifts well. Just as we would care for a gift someone gave us for our birthday, so we safeguard what God has given to us.

1. Make a list of some of the ways in which you might hold your work in high esteem and be grateful for it. Some suggestions include:

   • Acknowledging your gifts and talents and regularly taking time to thank God for them

   • Recognizing any positive characteristics of your colleagues and customers

   • Using your gifts only for the good of the whole, rather than for personal gain

- Balancing your work with other activities in life so that you have time to listen to God, your partner in work

2. Begin to practice gratitude for your work by implementing one or two of the suggestions on your list. Add others to your practice as you are comfortable doing so.

Seek Your Vocation

"Discover for yourself what seems to be the most fruitful field for you."

—Rule for a New Brother

You've probably heard the word "vocation" before. If you were raised in a Christian environment you probably learned that the word applied to the priest or minister of your church and to the nuns and monks in convents and monasteries. These people were called by God to do special work— God's work. God earmarked them for the job and made sure they knew they were called. What you may not have learned is that you, too, are called. You have a vocation, whether you know it or not.

However, a vocation is not a call to be a priest, minister, monk, or nun specifically. It is a call to work that God has set aside for you, that God calls you to do. That task or job enables you to become cocreator with God. You become God's hands or mouth here on earth, participating in the ongoing task of creating the world God plans for us.

Perhaps you think this doesn't apply to you. Maybe you work as a receptionist answering phones all day and that doesn't seem terribly exalted. Perhaps you build houses or pave streets or sell newspapers. A doctor or a nurse, a psychologist—now those people might have vocations. But how does it help God when we answer the phone or run the cash register?

I've worked in lots of offices and stores in my life, however, and I've seen many people who were called to the jobs of answering phones, helping customers, and running the cash register. How they exercise those tasks sometimes makes a tremendous difference in the lives of those they serve. One cashier that I knew always took time to really listen to the question a customer was asking and went out of her way to be extraordinarily helpful to everyone, even very difficult people. She learned the names of regular customers and many people came in just because they knew this cashier would smile and lend a sympathetic ear when needed. She made the store a more cheerful place to be. Aside from the fact that people simply enjoyed being in the store, and that was gift enough, it was also good for business.

In my own life I've learned the difference between listening to God, following the call I hear, and choosing to follow my own ego in pursuing career opportunities. Almost every job I've ever taken came about as the result of a sixth sense or intuition—my experience of call—that told me to take a particular position. When I've listened, the jobs have been the right ones at the right time. Even when the work has been very difficult, I knew I was in the right place doing the work I was meant to do. Only once did I take a job without listening for that sixth sense: I was listening instead to my own ego. The job was a disaster and I was a failure in it. I was grateful to get out of it after eighteen months of real misery.

You may well be in a job that is not your vocation right now. If you come home at the end of each day exhausted, angry, frustrated and tense, chances are you are not where you need to be. If it is possible you may need to seek a new job. Another possibility, however, is that you are just where you are called to be and if you listen more carefully you can discern what God asks of you in this situation. One way to do this is to begin each day with a short prayer to remind yourself to look for clues and to ask for God's guidance and help. This prayer from the Episcopal Book of Common Prayer is one I've found helpful. You might even write this prayer, or another one you find helpful, on an index card and keep it in your desk or your pocket during the day as a reminder of your intention to look for God's call throughout the day:

Almighty God our heavenly Father, you declare your glory and show forth your handiwork in the heavens and in the earth: Deliver us in our various occupations from the service of self alone, that we may do the work you give us to do in truth and beauty and for the common good; for the sake of him who came among us as one who serves, your Son Jesus Christ our Lord, who lives and reigns with you and the Holy Spirit, one God, for ever and ever. Amen.[18]

Practice

1. One of the ways to discern what God calls you to do is to watch each day for ways in which you can be of service to others and for opportunities to create rather than destroy. Maybe there is a kind word you can say, or a way to make "the system" work better for a particular individual. Perhaps by remembering

that you are acting on God's behalf you will build a
better house or gadget. Or by looking for God in all
those with whom you come into contact you will
make a difference in the day or life of one of God's
other children.

2. You may find it helpful to keep a journal of your
   observations each day. Write down all the ways in
   which you felt you were of service to anyone and
   the things you took particular joy in doing. As the
   pages fill up patterns will likely appear that can help
   you recognize God's call for you in your own particular situation. If you are truly someplace that is
   not for you, you may also begin to see what is missing from those journal pages and use that as a clue
   to help you find someplace more appropriate when
   that is possible.

Pray While Working

"They must do this [work faithfully and devotedly] in such a way that, while they banish idleness, the enemy of the soul, they do not extinguish the Spirit of holy prayer and devotion to which all other things of our earthly existence must contribute."

—The Rule of St. Clare

This rule reminds us that contemplation and action are not opposites. Rather, they complement one another. Contemplation without action (or work) too often becomes simple navel-gazing and ignores the needs of the world. Action without contemplation or prayer tends to be work that is to our own glory, without any consideration of God's desires for the world.

Perhaps you do not think of your work as an activity that makes a difference in God's developing world. But in most monastic communities work is held up as being of equal importance to prayer, worship, hospitality, and other practices. "By doing part-time work . . . you will remind the world more by deed than by word of the parallel values of prayer, generosity, silence, the brotherly life, peaceful hospitality and worship, and that we have always to seek first the Kingdom of God and his righteousness,"[19] says The Jerusalem Community Rule. All of these activities are equal because they are all ways of participating in the continuing creation of the world God—and each of us—hopes to see someday. We are being called in our work, as well as in other activities that have traditionally been labeled as spiritual, to be cocreators with God. If we are to be cocreators with God in this world, we must take the time through prayer and contemplation to listen to the desires of God our partner. In doing that, our actions in the world will be more meaningful.

Prayer can, for instance, help us discover a solution to a problem that confronts us in our work. There is nothing wrong with using our reason and the other skills we possess to overcome obstacles; these abilities are gifts God gave us and we are meant to use them fully. There is an old joke about a man who prays to God endlessly that he might win the lottery. Finally God tires of the man's prayers and says to him, "So why don't you buy a ticket already?" God cannot help us if we are unwilling to take action. Prayer is another tool or gift we have and one we often neglect when we are up against a deadline or facing a difficulty that seems insurmountable.

Not long ago I was trying to prepare for a presentation I had agreed to give and for several months I tried to figure out what I was going to say at the conference. Not a thing came to me, no matter how much I read or how much I thought about the topic. After complaining about this to my spiritual director one day, she looked at me and inquired about whether I had prayed about this speech. Rather sheepishly, I realized I hadn't. Prayer was the one thing I hadn't done and it provided the seeds that helped me to create the presentation I needed to make.

Prayer may also be the thing that helps us stay focused on bringing hospitality and generosity into the workplace. Part of the work of many monasteries is to offer hospitality to travelers or those who wish some retreat time. Monks and nuns do this by offering a clean, quiet place to stay and meals, along with invitations for visitors to join the community in prayer. Their wish to do all of this graciously comes out of their own prayer life and from the reading of Scripture. God calls them to the work of hospitality. Our way of being gracious and generous with those with whom and for whom we work—whether that be keeping a home for our family, in an office situation, or in manual labor—may be different from what a monastery offers. But prayer keeps us mindful of the fact that God exists in each person with whom we interact. Our responses to those around us are best when they reflect that knowledge.

Practice

There are many easy ways to remind ourselves of the need to pray about our work as well as incorporate prayer into our work life.

1. Find someplace in your work area where you can post a short prayer that you will see regularly. The prayer can be any that suits you. One particularly nice phrase from the Bible is "May the words of my mouth and the meditations of my heart be acceptable in your sight, O Lord, my rock and my redeemer."

2. Frame your day with prayer concerning your work. In the morning, before beginning your tasks, pray to be aware of God's presence throughout the coming day. At lunchtime, stop for a few minutes before eating and remind yourself of this intention once again. At the end of the workday take a few moments to thank God for whatever opportunities have come your way that day.

3. Take some time at the end of each workday to review your actions and activities. Which ones seemed to you to further the work that God sets out for us? Which ones did little or nothing to bring about a better world? Give thanks for those ways in which you participate with God in creating a better world and ask forgiveness for the things that were not helpful. Ask for God's help in healing whatever motivates or forces you to be destructive and seek to rectify the situation when possible.

Listen for the Wisdom of
the Community

"At least once a week the Abbess is required to call her sisters together in Chapter . . . There . . . she should consult with all her sisters on whatever concerns the welfare and good of the monastery; for the Lord often reveals what is best to the lesser [among us]."

—The Rule of St. Clare

In our highly individualistic culture it is easy to assume that each of us has all the required resources for figuring out what needs to be done and how it should be accomplished. Sometimes we truly are the right person to determine these things, but more often than not we might benefit from listening to views that differ from ours. This can become particularly important in the workplace, where power struggles often occur. We see one piece of the puzzle, while a colleague sees another. Perhaps our supervisor sees still more pieces and only God sees the whole. We will probably never see the whole that God sees in this life, but we can come closer to that vision when we take the time to listen to as many viewpoints as possible. Sometimes the community around us can provide far more than we will ever be able to grasp on our own.

Far too often in the business world, power is hierarchical. The person "at the top" is ultimately responsible for any decisions made or actions taken, so that person determines what will be said or done in a company. It is the corporate version of a childhood drama, where the mother tells a child he or she will do what is requested "because Mom said so." Mom—or the boss—is the undisputed authority and that is all the reason we are supposed to need in considering any course of action.

The Quakers, on the other hand, have a different model for understanding what God may be directing. Their Clearness Committee, a group of people gathered to help in discernment, seeks to help an individual or group determine what they are called to do or be simply by asking questions and listening to the responses. If, for instance, a person cannot seem to choose between staying in a current job or taking a new one, he might assemble a group of people he trusts and for two hours he will listen to the questions they ask, responding as truthfully as possible. The committee offers no advice and no suggestions. The members simply ask questions that help the person to consider all angles and get in touch with his or her deepest feelings and callings. Even the most conflicted person often exits a Clearness Committee with a strong sense of clarity and the ability to move forward.

Most of us are not in a position to establish clearness committees at work, but we can take some of the principles involved and use them individually. Many of us, for instance, when sitting in a meeting have witnessed or been a party to two or more people arguing for their individual points of view. Often the two people or groups involved fail to actually listen to each other and each simply continues to put forth its viewpoint without considering compromise or change. Neither group considers that the other group, looking at the issue from a different vantage point, might see something that it is missing.

It is more difficult to ask questions and consider other viewpoints than it is to push our own opinions. In order to do so we have to give up our need to be right and to win. We have to be willing to believe that others have a perspective that contributes to the development of the whole, even when that replaces our own viewpoint and hopes. That isn't always easy in a business world that rewards us for being the best and the brightest, but that was never the point of the Gospels anyway. Jesus did not reward the best and the brightest; in fact, he often put them in their place. By opening ourselves up to the wide variety of ideas and perspectives that come from others at work we are affirming that we are all children of God, that each of us sees a particular corner of God's world. By listening and learning about a corner that you have not seen before, you may even come to glimpse more of God's plan for the whole.

Practice

Rather than perpetuating the win-lose arguments in your life, decide to make a spiritual practice of asking questions and exploring viewpoints fully before making up your mind about something. The next time you find yourself in a situation where you are trying to get your own way at the expense of someone else try some of the following:

1. Try to set aside what you want for the moment. You can always come back to that later.

2. Ask questions. Like a journalist, see if you can discover the "who, what, why, when, where, and hows" of the conflict.

3. Take the time to consider how the other person's or group's viewpoint is helpful. What parts of it fit with your own? Is compromise possible? Is there a way for everyone to "win"?

Practice Careful Stewardship

"On Monday [the monks] hand over to others who take their place the vessels and utensils with which they have ministered, which these receive and keep with the utmost care and anxiety, that none of them may be injured or destroyed, as they believe that even for the smallest vessels they must give an account, as sacred things, not only to the present steward, but to the Lord."

—The Twelve Books of John Cassian on the
Institutes of the Coenobia

In the ancient monasteries of John Cassian's day monks took turns serving the rest of the community. Their duties included cooking, serving the food, or reading at meals. (Meals in monasteries were often silent with a solitary monk reading from a sacred book while the rest of the monks ate.) The tools that a monk would need—cooking and serving utensils, food, books—were scarce and anyone who damaged or destroyed one of them was severely punished. These tools were vital to the community's ability to do its work of serving God, hence they were sacred. Great care was taken, therefore, to preserve them and pass them intact to the next monk.

In our contemporary society where so many things are disposable or easily replaced, it is probably hard to imagine severe punishment for breaking a serving spoon. But Cassian goes on, in his rule, to tell the story of a steward finding three lentil beans that the monk on duty that week had let drop to the floor. Cassian reports that the monk was judged by the abbot to be a "pilferer and careless about sacred property, and so was suspended from prayer." The explanation for this severe punishment was a simple one, according to Cassian: "For they believe not only that they themselves are not their own, but also that everything that they possess is consecrated to the Lord."[20] John Cassian is telling us to take care of all our tools—how we use them and what we do with them matters a great deal to God.

What would it mean for you to think of your work and the tools of your work as things deserving of great care? Perhaps you work for a business and succeeded someone else who left your position. Someone will also follow you when you leave. How the job was done before you made a difference in how you do the work now. If your predecessor left the work in poor shape, you were probably forced to deal with cleaning up and starting over. If you do your work poorly, then the person who succeeds you will have to do the same. You are the steward—the caretaker—of your particular position for now. How you treat the work, your colleagues, and clients, makes a difference in your own life, in the lives of those around you, and ultimately to God.

Practicing stewardship today also involves care for the

tools of your work. Perhaps it means recycling paper, toner cartridge, or other items you use at work. If you are in a position of spending the company's money, you do so carefully and within the budget. It could also mean that you are a careful steward of your time and the time of others. You use your own time wisely, show up on time for meetings, and, when you can, avoid disturbing others who are busy.

Stewardship also involves taking care of relationships at work. For most of us there is not an inexhaustible supply of customers or clients. Even if there were, it takes less energy to treat current ones well and have them spread the word that you have been of service to them than it does to combat a poor reputation. It is also easier, in the long run, to work well with colleagues than it is to fight constant battles. And practicalities of business aside, if we go back to the story in Cassian's rule, we are reminded that all things, and that includes all people, are consecrated to God. We are good stewards when we become mentors and pass on what we have learned. We can serve customers, clients, and colleagues as we would serve God, for God lives within them as within us. We are only here temporarily to care for these things and these people. How we do that will make an enormous difference to God and to those who come after us.

Practice

If you would like to be a better steward of the work entrusted to you, you might begin by making a list of the ways in which you can do that. List the four categories mentioned above—tools, money, time, and relationships—and see if you can find one or more ways in which you might take better care of what is yours to safeguard. If your list is long you might begin by implementing just one or two items, gradually adding the other items on your list as you develop stronger habits of stewardship.

Admit Your Limits

"If the community is rather large, [the cellarer] should be given helpers, that with their assistance he may calmly perform the duties of this office."
—The Rule of St. Benedict

In a culture that celebrates profit and productivity, where owners, managers, and shareholders constantly demand more of their companies and workers, it can be hard to admit that there are limits to what each of us can accomplish. We all know people who work endless hours a day and even seven days a week in order to do the impossible—to prove that they are the best and most competent. In some professions that behavior is even expected and encouraged until one reaches a senior level and can relax just a little. But as much as we might like to produce to fill or exceed all expectations, we have bodies, minds, and souls that have limits. They give out when we push too hard for too long, often in dramatic and very inconvenient ways.

Instead, says Benedict, if the work is too much for one

person, let him (or her) have help. The cellarer in early monasteries was the person who handed out the supplies and food and generally kept track of the resources of the monastery. If the monastery was large that could be a huge task, more than one man could reasonably be asked to accomplish. So the cellarer was to be given helpers.

A little later in the rule Benedict says that the cellarer should be given help so that "he may calmly perform the duties of his office." How often do each of us "calmly perform" our work duties? Sometimes we pride ourselves on how busy and frantic we are. The more we have to do, the more messages we have to return, the more papers on our desk, the more often we are paged the better we feel. We take pride in not having a single moment to ourselves all day, in being breathless and harried (but still competent). If we happened to take a little time for ourselves or found a few hours of vacation on a business trip, we are quick to cover that up and assure others that we barely had time to breathe. There seems to be no greater sin in the work world than having time to "calmly perform our duties."

So what would happen if we actually stopped for a few minutes once in a while and gave ourselves time to think? If we moved toward a more contemplative way of being? Think about how different the workplace would be if we took time to engage with our customers or colleagues, to hear their stories and meet their needs. Or if we were relaxed enough to focus closely on the task at hand and give it the best of our attention instead of dealing with it peripherally. We have limits and we can only do so much at a given moment or on a given day. And what we choose to do and how we choose to do it makes a tremendous difference for our spiritual lives and for the lives of those around us. We can choose to do only what makes us look good or we can seek to do what we have been assigned or what serves God and others to the best of our ability.

Practice

One way of recognizing our limits is to set some boundaries for ourselves. By establishing some guidelines for the hours we will work, what we will do, and how we will serve, we admit to our limits and build them into our days.

1. Identify one thing about your work habits that seems to be either excessive in some way or not of service to God and others around you. Perhaps you routinely work too many days a week, ignoring your body's need for rest and recreation—and your friends or family in the process. Or maybe you forget to show hospitality to others around you at work, getting caught up in your own needs to the exclusion of others' concerns. Some of us also simply take on more and more, trying to prove we are superhuman, rather than saying "no" occasionally, asking for help, or delegating to others when appropriate.

2. Set some limit on the habit you've chosen to modify. Choose something manageable, not impossible, and do it just for a couple of weeks. Most of us can do most anything for a short period of time. Maybe the change is deciding to work six days a week instead of seven or saying "no" once during the two weeks. Perhaps we set ourselves a goal of listening to the concerns of one other person each day. Make it simple and something that you can actually measure.

3. If at the end of two weeks you are still struggling to accept the limit you set, resolve to try working on it for an additional period of time. Once you have learned to work with this new limitation, take some time to evaluate the difference it makes in your work. Are you more relaxed and thus able to work more efficiently? Do you feel more focused? Are you feeling more connected to clients, customers, or colleagues? Does recognizing the God-given limits in your life free you in any way?

4. Most of us who work too hard have more than one bad work habit to break. Those who work six or seven days a week probably also work ten to twelve hours a day or skip lunch and find themselves too busy and stressed to respond fully to those who surround them. When we first begin to cut back on work it is not at all unusual to feel guilt about giving less than we did in the past. Try to bear with it and know that God created rest and recreation as well as work. Repeat this exercise as often as is necessary to begin accepting that we are not God and that in order to keep God at the center of our lives we must make space for that to happen.

Refrain from Harsh Words
and Thoughts

"At work, they [monks] shall talk of no worldly matter,
but either recite holy things or else keep silent."
                              —The Rule of Pachomius

I t is hard to imagine the office or other work environment
without gossip. We gather around the coffee machine on
Monday morning to find out what others did over the weekend. We need to find out who is seeing whom and who did
something exciting during the last couple of days. Then
throughout the week, stories circulate about the latest successes and failures of other staff members. Quietly in corners
people whisper, "Did you hear about so-and-so?" Some of
the conversation is friendly and builds community, but far
too easily we move off into words that hurt and destroy instead.

It is also easy to indulge ourselves in harsh thoughts about
those with whom or for whom we work—we don't like our

boss or someone seems to be stepping on us as they climb the corporate ladder. Someone else is slacking off and we end up picking up the load. Or perhaps it is a client or customer who drives us mad. Mean-spirited words and thoughts seem to come so naturally to us in these situations.

But I witnessed the power of refraining from malicious talk recently while on a group tour of a foreign country. Whenever you commit yourself to spending a couple of weeks with twenty strangers, you can be reasonably assured that there will be friction among at least some members of the group. That was true during my vacation—there was someone in the group who many found difficult. Gossip happened here and there. Perhaps it even functioned as a way of blowing off steam that prevented more major confrontations. But one member of our group simply refused to join in the conversation. It was clear that she was experiencing some of the same difficulties, but she did not find it worthwhile to discuss them or to dwell on them. She was no Pollyanna. She acknowledged some of the problems briefly, but then she moved on. She saw the situation for what it was, but she saw no value in saying harsh words. Her focus was on the trip and her enjoyment of the time. Her silence and unwillingness to engage in malicious conversation was an important witness to the rest of us.

If for no other reason perhaps we learn to refrain from harmful gossip and conversation for our own sake. Repeating gossip or speaking ill of others without the intention of acting to change the difficult situation often leaves me feeling that I am not in right relationship with God anymore. By belittling one of those that God loves, I am essentially telling God that I know more than he does. I am losing the chance to work constructively with a difficult person or situation and denying myself the possibility of making a difference.

This does not mean that we never speak honestly, and even with anger, about situations or decisions that seem wrong to us. God does not ask us to lie down and take abuse or subject ourselves to unfair treatment. We are, however, asked to speak those angry words with the understanding that we are speaking to someone else who is beloved of God. We speak hard truths or angry words out of a genuine desire for justice, rather than to do damage to others.

Practice

Gossip comes so naturally to most of us that the first step in curbing our tongues is often becoming aware of the harsh things we say in a given day. Try the following, based on a traditional practice called the Prayer of Examen, as a way to begin to refocus your words at work:

1. Take time at the end of the day to look over the harsh words you said during the course of the day. These can be words you said directly to someone or gossip you repeated behind someone's back. Pay attention to how you feel about having said these things. Think back, too, to how you felt when you actually said whatever was hurtful.

2. Consider whether these hurtful actions are in accordance with the way that God asks you to live. Have you really "done unto others" as you want them to do for you?

3. If you have feelings of remorse for the things you've said, ask God to forgive you, and to help heal you of the need to say hard things. Ask God to be especially present with you through the day, helping

you to avoid gossip and malicious conversations. If you are faithful to this practice, you will pay attention to the number of hurtful things you've said or done, the feelings these actions create in you, and the consequences of these words on others. Subsequently, it is likely that you will begin to find yourself engaging in these activities less often.

Measure Success with Humility

"And although each one of them may bring in daily by his work and labour so great a return to the monastery that he could out of it not only satisfy his own moderate demands but could also abundantly supply the wants of many, yet he is in no way puffed up, nor does he flatter himself on account of his toil and this large gain from his labour."

—The Twelve Books of John Cassian on the Institute of the Coenobia

In all likelihood you've seen the scene in a movie or two where the boss takes credit for someone else's suggestion. The CEO comes in and heartily thanks the boss for an idea that has saved the company a client, or perhaps time and money. Rather than naming the originator of the idea the boss simply takes the credit and climbs one more rung on the corporate ladder. We do our own version of that every time we allow ourselves to be "puffed up" with our own success. If we view our work as a gift from God and God as a partner in our work, we cannot take all the credit when something works out well.

That does not mean that we can take no pride in a job well done. Certainly we played a part in the success of a project we worked on. We are not puppets controlled by God, moving our arms and legs only as the puppeteer allows. Nor does God demand that we be dour people who, like Ebenezer Scrooge in Dickens's *A Christmas Carol*, never enjoy a moment of our success. But as cocreators with God, we always work in partnership and the pleasure we find in a task completed well or a successful new idea belongs to the team as a whole, not to us individually.

Even if we leave God out of the equation, rarely are we solely responsible for a successful maneuver at work. We may have had a good idea, but in all likelihood others helped to flesh it out or implement it. An architect may design a beautiful house, but it takes contractors and craftspeople of all varieties to make that house a reality. Avoiding being puffed up by our own success means that we acknowledge the contributions of the whole team. We try to avoid claiming success at the expense of others. Imagine how much stronger the whole team would become if we reimagine the movie scene above. Instead of the boss simply taking credit for another's idea, imagine the improvement in morale and production if the boss took the CEO over to the person who came up with the idea and gave credit where it was due. This is a signal to the entire staff that good ideas are acknowledged and rewarded and that the entire team can take pride in all of its members.

God, of course, does not need us to give him credit, as a staff person might need from a supervisor. This is an exercise in humility for us, not for God. Nonetheless, if we take all the credit for what is accomplished through our hands, we deny a part of our relationship with God, just as we deny our dependence on other people who work with us. We are essentially saying that we do not need God's guidance or help in our work. At some point, however, we are likely to find that this is incorrect.

The practice of taking one's successes lightly, however, can also be taken to an extreme that is just as dangerous spiritually as taking all the credit for our success. By not acknowledging compliments and allowing others to thank us for the good work we do, we run the risk of taking pride in our humility instead of our accomplishments.

Practice

The proper response to a compliment is always a sincere "thank you." God does not ask us to take no credit at all for accomplishments in which we have played a part. Along with accepting the compliment, however, we can also be aware of the help of God and others who made the accomplishment possible. Practice acknowledging the contributions of others.

1. If you are praised by your supervisor for something you did and others had a part in that work, make sure the supervisor knows.

2. Make sure your colleagues know their work was good or their assistance was appreciated.

3. Be grateful for the gift of your work and thank God each day for the successes—large and small—that have come your way.

CHAPTER SIX

Study

"Study is not done for mere curiosity for learning but because wisely ordered reading endows the mind with greater steadiness and serves as a basis for the contemplation of God in His Word."

—Hermits of Bethlehem

It is a basic human tendency. All too easily we see the world through our own lens, assume that what we see is truth, and wonder how others can possibly view it from a different angle. Our lens is unavoidably shaped by the country and city we live in, the institutions that are a part of our life, and the families and environment in which we grew up and live. What we see, based on our own experiences, seems so clear and logical to us, tempting us to think that if others in the world only saw things as clearly as we do everything would run more smoothly than it does at the moment. Consciously or unconsciously we can find it hard to avoid thinking that our own lens should guide the vision of others.

One way to broaden our vision and begin glimpsing other truths is through study. When we read books, watch movies and television, listen to radio programs and lectures, attend classes, observe the world closely, and so on, we expose ourselves to new ideas and new ways of seeing that enlarge what we see and how we interpret what we encounter. It is certainly possible to censor materials and study only those resources that reinforce what we believe to be truth; it is even possible to study a wide range of resources but impose our own interpretations upon them to prevent them from challenging our own visions. But at its best, accessing a wide range of materials and looking at information with an open and receptive mind challenges all our deeply cherished notions, assumptions, and prejudices, including those about who God is and what God asks of us in this life.

For instance, while working on this book I read an overview of Christian spirituality, beginning in the earliest centuries and continuing up into the middle of the twentieth century. The author traced the development of the Christian search for God through writers, some of whom valued the mind and reason while others tended to give more credence to experience and feeling. Some thought it was necessary to empty ourselves of all distractions in order to make room for God (called the apophatic tradition) while others advocated a more imagination-oriented method of meditation (the kataphatic tradition). Many, of course, combined elements of both of these things. My own leanings tend toward feeling and experience and toward imagination rather than emptying, but through the reading of this book I gained additional insight into those who see the spiritual journey toward God differently than I do.

The same happens when we read books from those outside our own native culture, race, ethnic group, or sex. As a white, middle-aged woman raised in the U.S., how I imagine God will vary enormously from how a black young man raised in

Africa understands God. How someone from a Christian background understands God will be different than how someone who has been raised Jewish or Muslim understands God. And how we see God influences the way we speak to God and what we hear in response.

Studying other points of view, trying to look through different lenses, helps to move us from our own necessarily parochial perspective to contemplate other possibilities. It provides us with a broader basis "for the contemplation of God in His Word," or God in Her Word. New perspectives and new truths may not always be comfortable. At times we will find ourselves convicted of simple foolishness or immaturity or even of great wrongs. At other times we will find comfort, guidance, or encouragement. We never know what we will find in our studies, but what lies on each new page, in each class or observation, has the potential to show us a different facet of God and God's desire for us and for the world. Each thing that we learn from someone else brings us closer to others, to the ultimate truth, and finally to God.

Read Regularly

"Unless we grasp the truth that it is both a labor of love and a spiritual discipline, we are likely to neglect study. We should therefore support one another in regularly setting aside time for reading..."
—The Rule of the Society of St. John the Evangelist

In today's fast-paced world, where we've grown accustomed to getting much of our information in quick sound bites and by surfing the Internet at ever-increasing modem speeds, reading as a spiritual discipline may seem a little odd. Prayer is easily recognized as a spiritual practice and many of us can imagine that we might profit from spending more time at prayer. Few of us give much thought to spending more time reading and studying as a discipline. It isn't necessarily that we think poorly of these activities; it is, rather that we just don't think of them at all or not as part of our rule of life.

Reading, however, is a key way of encountering aspects of God that are unfamiliar to us. If we take the time to explore challenging reading—the Bible, the lives of the saints, books of spirituality or Bible study, poetry, fiction, etc.—we provide ourselves with the opportunity to expand our knowledge of God and God's activity here on earth. We may not agree with all that we read; in fact, we're probably not reading carefully if we never argue with any of the authors we read. It doesn't matter if we agree with someone or not, however. It is the opportunity to try on new ideas and perceptions that feeds not only our minds but ultimately our souls.

Maybe you were like I was when I was very young. I spent lots of my time at the public library reading book after book. I had an insatiable desire to read anything I could get my hands on. Fiction was one of my favorites and I had an endless fascination with various authors' abilities to create worlds that drew me away from my own. With my nose in a book, I was lost to the world for hours at a time. It would be decades before I realized that this kind of concentration and focus—this conversation with characters in a book—was very much like what I experienced in prayer and began to pay attention to reading as a spiritual discipline in my life.

Making time to read, especially material that makes you think, can be one of the most spiritually challenging activities you engage in. A friend of mine told me recently that she was reading a book about listening skills and came across the statement that giving someone the cold shoulder was a form of violence because it is done deliberately to inflict pain. She is one of the most gentle people I know, but we've all given someone the cold shoulder once in a while. She was shocked to think that she'd done something violent to another human being and resisted the author's statement for a while. Little by little, however, it crept into her thinking and feelings and she realized the author was correct in his assessment. Her spiritual life was profoundly challenged by what she had read and she no longer ignores people in that way. Her life was changed by what she read and yours may be, too.

Practice

If you decide to set aside a regular time for reading, the following suggestions may enhance your experience of this particular discipline:

1. Pay attention to the kinds of reading you feel drawn to and even the reading you find yourself resisting. If there are books or topics that "holler" at you and demand to be read, these can be good starting places. On the other hand, if you find yourself adamantly opposed to reading something, this may be a good time to wonder where your resistance comes from. Are you avoiding the book because you are afraid of what it contains, that it will challenge you in an uncomfortable ways? Perhaps you are basing your bias against the material on what others have said about it and not on your own experience. This is not to say that everything you don't want to read gets put to the top of your reading list, but pay attention to those books that you are actively resisting, as well as those that draw you in.

2. If you don't know where to start on your reading discipline, ask for help. Go to a bookstore or library and browse. Ask friends what they found engaging, challenging, or helpful. Spiritual directors or clergy can often help you, particularly if they know a little about you and your interests. Keep your options open and consider books in a wide variety of genres.

The books in the preceding categories are all good possibilities for your reading and are worth your consideration. But even something like religious murder mysteries (yes, there are lots of them on the market these days) can be very instructive and provocative. Many do a wonderful job of teaching the essentials of various faiths, sometimes raising important ethical and faith questions.

3. Try to read slowly and really engage in the material. Many of us are experts at getting things done quickly and efficiently, but spiritual reading is better suited to a slow speed that allows you to actively engage with the material. If it helps you to slow down, take notes or write in your journal about what you've read. Both strategies will give you some time to really think about what the author is trying to say.

4. It may be helpful to do your reading someplace where you won't be disturbed. If you decided to set up a prayer corner (see chapter 4) you may want to use it for spiritual reading as well. The prayers you say there and the sacredness of the space may deepen your reading.

Put Aside Times for Study

"During the days of Lent, [the monks] should be free in the morning to read until the third hour ... During this time in Lent each one is to receive a book from the library, and is to read the whole of it straight through. These books are to be distributed at the beginning of Lent."

—The Rule of St. Benedict

"What do you want to read for Lent this year?" a friend wrote to me online. Each year, for several years, we picked a book to study for Advent (the month or so before Christmas) and another for Lent and committed ourselves to reading each day, sending our thoughts to each other online. One of our favorite books to read took a scripture passage for each day and then used five or six pages of poems, prayers, and quotations from a variety of sacred and secular sources to explore the scripture passage from many different angles. As we read through it the first year I put small pencil marks next to the quotes that spoke most deeply to me. Then

I would send an e-mail to my friend each day, noting anything that had occurred to me. When we decided to read the book again a couple years later I was surprised to discover that some of the passages I'd marked no longer seemed special or important to me. The issues in my life were different and my relationship with God was deeper by the second reading, and that changed the way I experienced the various passages. Other quotations in the book were like old friends, and I discovered that I had been carrying them around with me for two years, letting them form and inform my spiritual life. Rereading the book gave me a bit of a marker of my own spiritual growth. It reminded me of the importance of study to my own maturation and the development of my friendship with God.

Though the electronic nature of that conversation may be new, the practice of reading and studying God's ways during these holy seasons is ancient. As early as the sixth century, Benedict's Rule suggested that the monks spend time reading—usually about two hours—every day of the year. On Sundays, except for worship, the entire day was spent reading or studying. During Lent[21], however, reading became even more focused and the monks spent three hours daily engaged in it. In addition, each was given a particular book from the monastery library to read during the holy Lenten period. Benedict does not write that the abbot selected just the right book for each person, but I can easily imagine the head of the monastery choosing a book for each monk, one that seemed to suit that man's spiritual needs at the moment.

For many individuals and in many churches today, the tradition of Lenten or Advent reading persists. Book groups often form for Advent and for Lent. A whole new crop of books written particularly for these holy seasons appears each year for use by individuals and study groups who want to commit themselves to studying God's word and ways as they prepare for Christmas or Easter. Some parishes practice a variation of this and invite members of the congregation to write brief devotional pieces for each day of the holy time and collect the writings into a booklet that gets distributed to the entire congregation.

Making a special effort to study during these times is certainly appropriate. Advent is a time of waiting and anticipation as we contemplate the birth of Jesus. Lent is a time of self-examination, or reorienting ourselves, in an effort to follow God's ways more closely. Observing these seasons fully involves special attention to prayer, to our spiritual disciplines, and an increased effort to pay attention to God's desires for us. Reading the scriptures and the words of those who are meditating upon them helps us stay more focused and present to God during these special times. Those whose regular daily schedules make reading and study difficult often find that adopting this discipline for the four weeks before Christmas and the forty days (plus Sundays) between Ash Wednesday and Easter deepens their spiritual life enormously, not only during Lent and Advent, but all year long. Just as we celebrate the changing colors of the leaves or the first snowfall as ways of marking the beginning of a new season, the discipline of setting aside time for study marks these time periods as powerful spiritual seasons.

Practice

If making a commitment to study during Advent or Lent appeals to you, try some of the following suggestions:

1. Pick a book that fits your interests and schedule. You might decide, for instance, to read a portion of the

Bible each day. Maybe you will want to read one book of the Bible during the whole time period. You could also decide to follow the lectionary readings assigned by the church.[22] There are also many Advent and Lent books available from local religious bookstores. Any book that seems spiritually nurturing will be a good choice. Be sure to pick something that suits the time you have available each day. Deciding to read the entire Bible during Advent when you have fifteen to twenty minutes a day that you can give to reading is an exercise doomed to failure.

2. Make the commitment to read and study each day. For some, doing this at a set time each day works best. Others will find that they prefer to read whenever the spirit moves them to do so.

3. You might wish to use a journal in connection with your reading. Recording your thoughts about the day's passage helps many people retain the material better. The process of writing also brings thoughts to the surface that may surprise you.

4. A short prayer before reading, one that asks God to speak to you in the day's text, can deepen the experience and your connection to God. Likewise, praying at the end of your study time and thanking God for this time each day is appropriate.

5. Make the commitment to study with a friend or a book group if that seems helpful. Getting together with another person or a study group once a week

can help maintain the discipline of reading and allows you to hear other perspectives on the texts. Making a commitment to do this with an e-mail friend can accomplish the same things.

Meditate on God's Word

"You must not only be a hearer of the Word—you must also bring it to fulfillment. Happy are you if you meditate upon it daily in your heart. You will be like a tree by the running water, whose branches will stay fresh and green, and they will keep bringing forth new fruit."

—Rule for a New Brother

Have you ever had the experience of rereading a book you read as a child? Recently I reread the classic children's book *Wind in the Willows*. I had fond memories of the animals in the book from my childhood years, but when I read it again this year I discovered a whole different book. The cute and delightful animals I remembered from my earliest reading now took on characteristics of all sorts of people I've met in my life. I understood the satire and humor of the book and of the foibles of the various creatures much more clearly. What was a wonderful story many years ago now read as a study of human nature and values.

God's word is like that, too. What we heard in the Bible stories as a child is not what we will hear as an adult. And, because life constantly hands us new experiences, a given passage that I read even yesterday might strike me quite differently today. A Psalm that cries for God's mercy, for instance, will mean more to me in times of distress than it does when my life is going along easily. Change can happen when a very familiar phrase or word suddenly takes on new meaning for us on the twentieth reading of a passage. This is one of the ways in which God speaks to us if we choose to pay attention.

Perhaps such experiences were what prompted St. Benedict to create the process of *lectio divina*, or sacred reading, in the sixth century. He wrote an entire chapter forty-eight of his rule describing the times set aside for reading and the importance of it to the spiritual life. Over the centuries the practice has continued to develop and there are endless variations on how to read deeply, but the basic premise of *lectio divina* is that we take the time to read a small piece of scripture (or other sacred reading) slowly, looking within it for God's message to us.[23] There are three basic parts common to most ways of practicing *lectio divina*: We read slowly and deeply, then meditate on what we have read, and finally offer prayers to God based on what we have learned.

What we "hear" when we read deeply like this can surprise us. On a particular day God's words to us offer comfort or the strength to continue on a difficult journey. Other times what we hear helps us offer praise to God for the wonderful gifts we have received. During times of spiritual complacency the words we hear may even challenge or convict us, pushing us forward or asking us to change the way we live. The only thing we can count on when we practice spiritual reading is that, if we are truly seeking God's guidance, we will be given something that nourishes us. "You will be like a tree by the running water, whose branches will stay fresh and green, and they will keep bringing forth new fruit," says the Rule for a New Brother. *Lectio divina*, for many people, is the running water that provides the sustenance that makes the spiritual journey possible.

Practice

There are many different ways to read deeply and none of them is more correct than any of the others. All of the ways of practicing *lectio divina*, however, suggest that you read your chosen text slowly at least three or four times and focus on one activity or question each time. The text should not be a long one—not more than a paragraph or so generally—and can be from the Bible or from another book of spiritual reading. Lectionaries, or the assigned readings of churches for each day of the year, can be found in most denominational prayer books and they provide excellent sources for regular and methodical reading of the Bible. Once you have chosen a text, read it slowly before following three or four of the suggestions below:

1. Notice if any particular phrases or words jump out at you. Simply sit silent for several minutes (or longer if desired) and let that phrase or word rest in your thoughts.

2. Keep one of the following questions in mind as you read the text each time: You may want to record your answer to this and other questions in a journal.

   A. What meaning does this passage have for your life right now?

B. Does this passage challenge you to do anything differently?

C. Can you give thanks for anything you have heard in this passage?

3. Using a biblical commentary (if you are reading the Bible) look up your passage and learn more about its context and history. How does this information enrich your understanding of the passage?

4. Imagine yourself within the text. What character are you? What do you see around you? What feelings does the passage create in you?

5. Write a prayer as a response to the passage.

6. Using some kind of art materials (clay, paint, fabric, and so on) create something that is a response to what you have read.

7. If you are reading first thing in the morning, commit yourself to recalling this passage at various points of the day, letting it sink in more deeply as the day continues.

8. On the last reading, simply rest in the words and let them become part of you.

Study the Ancient Wisdom

"Learn from your companions and study how the saints
of God have prayed."

—Rule for a New Brother

U p until now in this chapter I have focused on reading
as a way of studying. Reading what others have written
is essential to our spiritual lives. There are so many wonderful explorations of spirituality available in books today—not
just the ones by the canonized saints of the church, but by
hundreds of contemporary writers who share their explorations of the place of God in their lives. There is much we can
learn from them, so many new insights and methods. But
studying and learning from others involves participation in
activities other than reading. Classes, workshops and semi-
nars, retreats, and pilgrimages also provide us with opportunities to study, to learn from some of the saints of God.
While some of these might involve reading as well, much of
what we learn comes from lectures, our own direct experi-

ences of new practices or places, and from interaction with other saints of God.

Recently I went on a two-week pilgrimage to southwest Ireland. The trip was led by someone who had studied the places we visited and who also brought in guest speakers who could tell us more about the people, the history, and even the flora and fauna of the various sites. Twenty-four of us tramped around in rain and sunshine—whatever the day brought us—climbing hills, walking ancient pathways, visiting ruins of churches, dipping into the water of holy wells, worshipping together on hills overlooking the Atlantic ocean. We shared stories of our lives and our impressions of these holy sites that thousands of others had visited over the centuries. We ate and laughed together, drank beer together late at night, played and shopped together, and we even spent one day in silence absorbing what we had seen and experienced, listening for the holy in all of it. We learned the history of the various sites, and we studied how the Celts had prayed centuries before us.

It was a time of communion with the ancient saints of God, both the ones for whom the various places were named, but also the thousands who had played and prayed in these spots, just as we were doing. The presence of the hundreds of thousands of prayers was palpable in many of the places we visited. But we also had the sense that we, as today's saints of God, were adding our own presence and prayers to what was already there, leaving those behind for future generations to experience.

These are the kinds of opportunities that open us to the wisdom of those who have come before us and to those who surround us today. By seeing the places where people have prayed for centuries, by participating in a pilgrimage trip, a retreat, or a seminar with others, we discover how others have seen, or see, the work of God on this earth, and broaden our own ability to see God at work in our lives and in the lives of those around us.

Practice

If studying in this way appeals to you, seek out educational opportunities that fit your schedule and budget.

1. Attend a retreat or pilgrimage that appeals to you. Almost any spirituality or religion-based magazine carries ads for a variety of retreats and pilgrimage trips to fit any schedule. You can also find resources on the Internet or by talking with friends or local clergy. Various retreat centers around the country offer weekend and weeklong retreats, often with well-known scholars or practitioners of the spiritual life. Pilgrimages, usually lasting ten days to two weeks, to almost any part of the world also abound.

2. Other options for studying a bit closer to home and less expensively can often be found in your local congregation. Sunday morning classes are a regular feature of many churches, as are occasional retreats that often focus on a particular theme or holy period. If you live in an urban area, chances are there are also some spirituality institutes, seminaries, or other organizations that also offer regular and inexpensive classes and workshops. All of these more local options have the advantage of connecting you with others in your own area who share your interests.

Learn from Others

"In the morning . . . after the prayers are finished they shall not return right away to their cells, but they shall discuss among themselves the instruction they heard from their housemasters."

—The Rule of Pachomius

There are very few positive references to speaking in most monastic rules. Far more common are the reminders to speak as little as possible and to use well-considered words when it is absolutely necessary to talk. Silence—being much harder to maintain than speech—is the desired monastic trait. So this rule from Pachomius is unusual, but a good reminder of the importance of discussing what we are learning with others as a way of studying God's wisdom for us.

When we come across something new in the spiritual life—whether it is something we read, hear, or see—we so easily assume that we have interpreted the one true meaning of what we encountered. So often we forget the ambiguous nature of most material; we forget that we view everything through our own particular lenses and that many other interpretations are also quite viable. I have a colleague, for instance, who is about as conservative as I am liberal. I spent twenty years in Berkeley, California, so he assumes I am flamingly liberal in my views. He comes from an evangelical background, so I often expect him to be very conservative. More often than not, we are both wrong. He loves to argue about politics, religion, and other controversial issues, so we do, in fact, find ourselves on opposing sides of issues often enough. Yet we have both been surprised to find that we agree with each other or that we have been swayed by the other person's viewpoint with some regularity. We had a lengthy discussion one day about being single in the church and found ourselves in perfect accord. But whether we agree or not, our conversations have given each of us new things to consider. Once we get past our assumptions about each other, we have been able to listen and challenge one another to consider new angles on issues and ideas we had previously taken for granted.

The conversations with my colleague remind me that the first and most important skill of a good conversationalist is the ability to listen. So often in talking with people we focus on pushing our own point of view; we want to be right and have the other person be wrong. Even before our partner in conversation has stopped speaking, we have stopped listening, and have begun formulating our counterarguments. When our turn to speak comes, we have spent so much time figuring out what we will say that we realize we have not even heard everything the other person said.

Another thing we are prone to is making assumptions about other people's points of view based on their appearance or what we have heard or already know about them. Both of these approaches make it hard to learn anything new or see things from a different angle. We are too intent on proving how clever we are or on getting our own way to learn from someone else. When we do this consistently we lose the opportunity to explore the richness and diversity of the world with which God surrounded us. We look only through our own lens, one that may be getting old and faded with age and use. Just as we need to see an optometrist regularly to have our eyesight checked, we need to talk with others to make sure that our "lens" is working well and allowing us to see everything in front of us. By listening to others and seeing through their lenses, our own study of God is deepened.

Practice

Many years ago I was introduced to the concept of a Quaker Circle. In this exercise, often used with groups, the leader asks a question and silence fills the room until someone feels moved to respond. Once the first person answers the question each person in the circle, going either in a clockwise or counterclockwise direction, is given time to respond. The only rule is that you cannot respond to anyone else's statements; no clarifications or arguments may be made. Because of this—because no response to any comments is permitted—everyone is freed from thinking about what they will say in answer to another and they can simply listen to what is being said.

1. Try this in your own conversations regularly. Simply listen to what your conversation partner is saying without trying to formulate a response or think of a story that illustrates his or her point, or argue another point of view. Just listen. When the other per-

son is done speaking you can take a few moments to form your thoughts and respond as needed. Those few seconds of silence may feel awkward to you at first, but the person to whom you are speaking will most likely recognize that you are seriously considering what he or she said before answering and will realize that you are truly listening to what they have said.

2. When you have time to reflect on the conversation later, consider the following questions:

- How did your careful listening affect you? How did it affect the other person who was talking?

- Did you learn something new? See a new way?

- How might God have been speaking to you in the conversation?

Study All of God's Creation

"Our pursuit of knowledge is an expression of love for God's world and the riches of revelation. As we bring our gifts of imagination and intellect to maturity we are able to glorify God more and more."
—The Rule of the Society of St. John the Evangelist

When we think about study in connection with religion and a rule of life, usually we think of studying the Bible. That is certainly important and several of the other sections in this chapter address that kind of study. But we can glorify God and learn more about God's creation in any number of ways, not only through books but in observing the world more closely.

A friend of mine who I'll call Karen told me once of a day she spent with her cousin walking around in the wilderness. Her cousin, who was very knowledgeable about botany, nearly drove Karen crazy by naming all the plants they saw and providing details of their growth habits. Karen, who was simply enjoying being out walking finally got exasperated and asked her cousin why she had to name everything she saw. The answer was a surprise: knowing the names of everything was a sign of respect for the plant and ultimately for creation itself. The story reminds me of Adam naming the animals in Genesis. By studying all the animals and providing them with names, Adam was using his "gifts of imagination and intellect" to glorify God.

Not too long ago a friend of mine began teaching me about watching birds. I knew what a robin was and was familiar with a few other birds, but I had no idea of the variety of them in creation until recently. Intrigued by their beauty I finally bought a guidebook to help me identify individual breeds of birds and I've spent hours poring over the book trying to learn the names of the various birds I've seen on my walks. There is something sacred about this reading, just as there is about the time I spend with Scripture. It is, for me, a way of learning more about and appreciating God's world.

The observation of the birds has also become sacred time for me. To watch birds you must move slowly and be very quiet. Often you have to just stand still and wait in a place that might be a likely bird habitat. More than once I have found myself in prayer in such a place, watching quietly for God's presence as I wait for the birds. And while waiting I have learned to notice more of what is around me—the fish in the water, the trees, the sun, or rain. I am learning to "read" God's creation more deeply.

Lectio divina, the ancient practice of sacred reading, involves reading a small amount of text meditatively, seeking every ounce of meaning the passage can possibly provide. But we can also practice lectio by "reading" God's creation in order to know God better. Our study of all God's creations is an expression of our love of God and our thanksgiving for all that we have been given. Perhaps practicing *lectio divina* on those things we find in nature can help us appreciate the whole creation of which we are just one small piece. The *Plan of Life,* or book of rules for the contemporary Hermits of Bethlehem speaks clearly of this:

> "God speaks to us through His marvelous creation, the things He made, the world of nature ... Let creation be for the hermit a book of learning about God, a book by which the mind feeds on the bread of creation. ... Take notice of the birds and the animals, smell the flowers, walk in the woods, smell the pine, listen to the brook, take a leaf, touch a rock, watch the sunset, look up at the stars, feel the raindrops and snowflakes, listen to the rhythm of your body, your heartbeat. They speak of God leading one into silent adoration of the All-wise and Holy Creator."[24]

Over the last few years I have found that objects from nature have a great deal to teach me about God and prayer. One rock, in particular, continues to teach me about silence and peacefulness. I picked it up on a silent retreat years ago and it fits perfectly in the palm of my hand. It even has a ridge that fits under my curled-up fingers as the rock rests in my palm. When I first pick it up it is usually cool to the touch and it warms as I hold it. It feels solid to the touch, and is a dull, ordinary brown. But it is smooth—worn down by years of desert sands. The rock brings back memories of a deep peacefulness and sense of connection to God that I felt on the retreat where I found the rock. Its smoothness speaks to me of resilience, of something worn by what is around it, but which has become smooth in the wearing. I hold it when I need to be reminded to let myself be shaped by whatever forces press against me, when I need to find some peacefulness in the midst of chaos. In its own way, this hard rock teaches me about flexibility and peacefulness, about letting God wear us down into the shape we were meant to assume.

Practice

The following exercise, practiced regularly can help us notice and study more deeply:

1. Pick an object you would enjoy looking at for a half hour or longer. A flower, a rock, a tree, or some other object that is stationary works best. (Animals, who will probably run, swim, or fly away usually don't work well.) If you wish, you might do a little reading about the object you've selected—the type of plant or rock, and whatever else you can learn about it. This is not necessary, but can increase your appreciation for the unique qualities of the particular item.

2. Quiet yourself in whatever way works best for you. As much as possible clear your mind of distractions and try to become aware of where you are sitting and what is around you.

3. Focus on the object you have selected. If it is possible you might want to use as many senses as possible to learn about it—touch, smell, sight, taste if it is safe to do so, and sound if one is associated with the item. Keeping your mind as clear as possible, let the object speak to you through your senses.

4. Now try to deepen your study of the object. Did your research uncover anything that instructs you in

any way? Does the item's struggle to survive, or its beauty, or its environment say anything specific to you? Does its strength or fragility teach you anything? How might God be speaking to you through this object? Spend as much time as you wish with this, perhaps writing down your observations in a journal.

5. As you come to the end of your meditation, focus on how you can respond to your object and to God. Is there a prayer you wish to say? Or a promise you want to make to God?

6. Finally, give thanks for the lessons you have learned from another part of God's creation. If appropriate, return the item to its natural environment and give thanks for the temporary loan.

CHAPTER SEVEN

Spiritual Community

"I consider that life passed in company with a number of persons in the same habitation is more advantageous [than solitary living]."

—The Long Rules of St. Basil

When America was a young country it based its constitution and political philosophies on something very important: It named and safeguarded the rights of many of the individuals who populated the new territory. As a nation, we continue to hold that dear and, when we are at our best, strive to protect the rights of all people. Somewhere along the way, however, we went too far, and the individual became more important than the whole. Many of us began to believe that we—at least from teenage years on—could determine our own path, guide ourselves through life, without feedback, training, and help from others. In the sixties, when I was a teenager, I remember one of my favorite refrains went something like this, "As long as I'm not hurting anyone else, it doesn't matter what I do."

Beginning in the 1960s many of us in the U.S. began to

believe that we could, as sociologist Robert Wuthnow put it, "negotiate our own understandings and experiences of the sacred."[25] As we became more aware of a variety of religious traditions, particularly the Eastern ones, people began to combine elements from a variety of religious perspectives (Native American, Eastern, Christian, Jewish, Buddhist, and others) to create their own belief structures and practices. This new awareness of traditions outside of Christianity opened many of us to a knowledge of, and appreciation for, a wide variety of religious understandings. At the same time, it encouraged a highly individualized practice of faith, one that was not always guided by the wisdom of others, and which provided little sense of community. The experience, for many, was valuable, but lacking in depth and commitment. As Wuthnow states, it resulted in "a transient spiritual experience characterized more often by dabbling then by depth."[26]

And while we think of this as a particularly American experience in the late twentieth century, it essentially bears a strong resemblance to the experience of many spiritual seekers in the Egyptian deserts of the fourth century, as we discussed in the first chapter of this book. Ultimately, individual and private religion will always be less than satisfying. By pursuing the sacred alone we can avoid the annoyances of being in community with people and ideas we don't always enjoy, but we lose the community's ability to challenge us to understand God more fully. Unless we have an accident or life goes dreadfully wrong for us, when we are our own guides we seek out only those images of God that please us and avoid ones that force us to rethink our views. And when we shape God in our own image, rather than letting ourselves be molded by the understandings of God held by the various members of our communities, our theology becomes self-centered, weak, and insubstantial.

Perhaps you have seen the popular children's book called *Old Turtle*.[27] In it, each animal and object argues that God is created in that animal's or object's image. The rock thinks God is solid and stable. The birds imagine God flying above everything. No one sees anything but their own characteristics in God and they argue incessantly about it, until Old Turtle begs them to stop fighting and teaches them that God is the sum of all their visions and more. When we live within community we give ourselves the opportunity to learn about the faces of God that we would not ordinarily see. It is in community that our image of God is tested and refined, where we are held accountable for what we believe and how we act, and ultimately where we meet God in the fullest possible way.

It is also within community that we find love and encouragement and support on the spiritual path. We find others who pray with and for us, who celebrate our lives and ask us to celebrate theirs. In community we find laughter as well as tears; we find people to play with, as well as ones who can mourn with us when times are rough. It may even be that we have gifts and skills that would not manifest themselves outside of community. By failing to use them or by hoarding them for ourselves, we misuse what God has so graciously given us.

To experience all of this, however, we must be willing to be open to the love of the community. "Be humble enough to let yourself be seen for what you really are, and understanding enough to see without judging," says The Jerusalem Community Rule of Life.[28] It takes tremendous courage, then, to live in spiritual community with others. But it is only in opening ourselves to that experience—to the many faces and characteristics of God that we find in other people of God—that the healing of the fragmentation of our society can begin. By allowing ourselves to be known by a spiritual director, a spiritual friend, a church community, or prayer group, and by taking the time to discover God in others, life is healed and sanctified, we find a better balance for our own lives, and we move one step closer to God's desire for this world.

Find a Worship Community

"Human beings were created to bless and adore their Creator and in the offering of worship to experience their highest joy and their deepest communion with one another. In our fallenness we continually turn in upon ourselves to seek fulfillment without self-offering . . . Worship makes costly demands on our time and energies. It calls us from the inertia of self-centeredness."
—The Rule of the Society of St. John the Evangelist

A few years ago I was a member of a wonderful women's prayer group that met monthly. We chose a monthly meeting because we all knew that we would never be able to organize our schedules to gather more often than that, despite our best intentions and the importance we placed on our prayer lives. Even with just the monthly meeting some evenings I found that I could invent half a dozen excuses for not attending. Since we met on a weekday evening I could plead fatigue from a long workday. Or I needed to prepare for the next long workday. The house suddenly needed cleaning or the cat needed some attention. Or there was a great program on television that night. There were many evenings when I had to force myself to go, but afterward I was never sorry for the effort.

The evenings I spent with that particular group of women were some of the richest spiritual experiences of my life. We experimented with a variety of prayer traditions, learning from one another. But we always left some time to check in with each other, giving each person some time to talk about what was going on in her life. We prayed over the problems of each person and offered comfort, support, or thanks as appropriate. The evenings helped me change my focus from my own fatigue or self-centered desires and be present, instead, to others who needed my attention. They also brought me face-to-face with how God was moving in my life and in the lives of the other women in the group.

In the rush of our daily lives we often fail to establish or join spiritual communities that focus us more clearly on God and move us away from self-centeredness. If you are an introvert, finding the nurturing communities and making the effort to be active within them can feel like one more thing on the "to-do" list, rather than a source of communion and deep joy. If, however, we attend to our spiritual life outside of community we miss a great deal. Left to our own devices we will develop a comfortable spirituality that fails to challenge us. Perhaps it will be perfectly crafted for our own needs, but leaves out those of others. More than likely it will be a weak theology that does not sustain us in times of deep trouble. Without the community we have little support when things go wrong in our world; without having developed the habit of nurturing as well as challenging others we will be without others to help us celebrate or mourn the important moments in our lives.

Being a member of a spiritual community is not always easy. If you've been a church member you know that church communities can divide a church, just as they do in the business world. Perhaps you've met the bossy matron who rules the church kitchen or the head usher who needs everything to be "just so." But you probably also met some of the church's gentler people—the ones who greet you warmly at the door or hug you during the passing of the peace during the worship service. Maybe you went to a new church once and some kind soul helped you find your way through the unfamiliar service and invited you to the coffee hour afterward. Churches, prayer groups, and other spiritual communities are full of people you will adore and people you'll find harder to love. But every one of them is beloved of God and reveals something of God for you to learn and know. Individually and collectively they invite you out of your own world and into the communion of the whole people of God.

Practice

1. If you are not already part of a spiritual community do some research on ones that are available in your area. Perhaps there is a church that might feel like home to you. A local bookstore might have a spirituality reading group. Or, if you live in an urban area, there may well be a seminary or religious or spiritual institutes of various sorts that offer classes or ongoing reading or prayer groups. If you can't locate an already existing group that seems right to you, consider gathering some of your friends and friends of friends and starting something of your own.

2. Make a commitment to be active and participate in the group in some way. Perhaps it is a class and your commitment will be to attend each of the meetings and be in conversation with others in the group. Maybe you will find a church you like and you can commit yourself to regular Sunday attendance or to a certain number of Sundays a month. Perhaps there are small groups within the church you may want to consider attending regularly. Stay with the promise of attendance and participation you've made for yourself and see what differences this commitment makes in your life.

3. You may want to keep a journal that reflects on some of the following questions:

   • What do you bring to the group? Are you able to put your own concerns aside sometimes and offer assistance to others?

   • What kind of obstacles do you find to regular participation in a group?

   • How do members of the group challenge your theology and spiritual understandings?

   • What are you learning from the people whose views differ from yours or from those who you find less appealing than others?

   • In what ways does this regular commitment enrich your spiritual life?

Observe the Seasons As a
Spiritual Journey

"You will find a source of wisdom and spiritual joy in the feasts of the Church. The year is crowned with the signs of God's goodness. If you celebrate these feasts with the Church then your own life and suffering, your enthusiasm and work, your dying and rising and your waiting for the Lord will receive significance and impact."

—Rule for a New Brother

Not too long ago I moved from California back to the East Coast where I grew up. I'd been in California for twenty years and I had forgotten how dramatic the change of seasons is in the East. I spent the whole first year watching, reacquainting myself with them. A hot and humid summer became a brightly colored fall. Then winter was upon us; the leaves fell from the trees and the world was gray for many months. Finally spring arrived and week by week flowers bloomed and the world came alive again. Watching the changes in the landscape was astonishing, but even more fascinating were people's reactions to the changes around them. The first day of real spring weather, for instance, brought everyone out of their houses where they had hibernated for the winter. The sound of people doing lawn work, greeting one another, and children playing together outside broke the silence of winter that day—all just in response to a little sunshine and warmth in the air.

The changing seasons mark large chunks of time for us, just as clocks and calendars mark hours, days, weeks, and months. And though we observe the movement of time in private and individual ways, it is the community marking of time and seasons that is the most dramatic. It is the neighbors talking over the back fence on the first warm day of spring, the parades and the picnics, and the gatherings of friends and families on holidays that most clearly mark the passage of the seasons. The Christian calendar has seasons as well, ones that mark an annual spiritual journey for us. Just as with secular holidays and seasons, the liturgical seasons, observed within community, take us more deeply into that community and ultimately into the heart of God.

The year begins with Advent, four Sundays before Christmas Day. This season, early in the winter, is a time of waiting and darkness. We await the return of the sun and warmth, but more important, we wait once again to experience the birth of Jesus, the Word made flesh. The Twelve Days of Christmas and then Epiphany follow Advent, and this is a time for celebration and feasting. The child Jesus has been born and is called Emmanuel or God-with-us. We celebrate God's presence come again in earthly form.

We have one final feast on Shrove Tuesday, also called Carnival or Mardi Gras. The next day Lent begins and this is a period of prayer and penance. Ash Wednesday starts a time of looking inward and of giving to others in need. Symbolically we wander in our own desert for the forty days of Lent, just as Jesus wandered in the desert before he began his public ministry. Lent ends with Holy Week, a time when we remember the crucifixion of Jesus and our own role in rejecting him again and again.

At the end of Holy Week, however, is Easter and we celebrate new life—the resurrection of Jesus. Hope, like spring, is born again. The celebration of the Easter resurrection ends on Pentecost, the time of Jesus' disappearance from the earth and the beginning of the Spirit incarnate in each of us. The long season after Pentecost, or Ordinary Time as it is called in some traditions, is broken only by All Saints' Day at the end of October, when we remember those who have died before us. A few weeks later we begin the cycle all over again.

It is a full spiritual journey throughout the year. We begin with hopefulness and expectation, which is fulfilled in the Christmas season. By the time Lent rolls around we discover, once again, that our faith has not been deep enough and we endure a period of contemplation and reflection. On Easter we experience new life once again, this time in a deeper way than we did on Christmas. Pentecost follows, and we are once again commissioned to go out and do the work of God. If we participate in this journey, our own involvement in it becomes deeper each time and we understand our place in God's world more fully year by year.

There are many different ways to join the spiritual journey of other Christians through the seasons of the year, but the Sunday and special services of the church is one of the best. The spiritual journey, though an individual one for each of us, needs the support of others who know the journey, something that churches can often provide. Most churches observe the various seasons by decorating the church in particular ways, singing the hymns appropriate to the time, and reading the stories from Scripture that are the basis of our journey. Just as we watch the landscape around us change during the fall, winter, spring, and summer, the church itself changes. Various colors mark the seasons in many churches, though there is variation from place to place. Blue or purple marks Advent, while white marks Christmas. Green or white comes out in Epiphany; a very dark purple characterizes the church in Lent. Red is the color of Pentecost, and then the church returns to green for the long season between Pentecost and the return of Advent.

There are also a variety of services that mark these special seasons and days. Even those who rarely go to church often attend on Christmas Eve and Easter Day and know the glory of those particular services. Fewer people know the services of Holy Week, which come from our most ancient traditions and speak deeply to the soul. Palm Sunday sets the stage for the week with a dramatic reenactment of the Passion story, the events that lead up to and include the crucifixion of Jesus. Various services follow throughout the week. All are rich services that help us connect with our own sense of wrong-doing and with mourning for what we have done and what has been lost. Each of the various church seasons has special services such as these that can help us stay on the journey.

Some churches also provide a variety of other activities around the various church seasons. Retreats are common during Lent and Advent. Special community potluck dinners and educational events occur in churches, as well as a variety of other opportunities. None of this precludes observing the seasons in ways that have significance to you as an individual; they are meant to supplement and support your own efforts, to provide guidance, encouragement, and companionship on the journey. By participating in some of them, by observing the seasons fully, we reconnect to our hopes and dreams, our errors and needs, or as Rule for a New Brother above says: our own life and suffering, our enthusiasm and work, our dying and rising.

Practice

1. Make a commitment to being present within a particular worship community for at least one year. Attend as many of the Sunday morning services as you can, as well as special services during Advent, Lent, and other special times of celebration. Pay attention to the ways in which this shapes your sense of time and of God's presence.

2. The church calendar intersperses periods of rest, waiting, and mourning with times of celebration and feasting. Each year there is also a long period of time from Pentecost (in early summer) through the fall (called Ordinary Time, as mentioned earlier) in some traditions, when there are no major holidays but during which the lectionary readings guide us through a variety of Old and New Testament events. How does this cycle affect your own rhythms?

3. How do the periods of waiting or self-reflection during Advent and Lent affect your sense of celebration at Christmas and Easter?

4. It may be easier to have a sense of God's presence during the major holy days of the church. Can you

still sense God with you during the long period of Ordinary Time?

5. What difference does it make to celebrate the cycle of the church year within community?

Take the Eucharist Regularly

"Christ, the Word made flesh, gives himself to us visibly in the Sacrament. Therefore nourish yourself with the meal of thanksgiving, the Holy Communion, and do not forget that it is offered to the sick of the People of God. It is there for you who are always weak and infirm."

—The Rule of Taizé

No matter how many times I witness this act and hear these words, I am awestruck. The priest raises the wine and the bread, presenting them to the congregation (always to the group, never the individual) and pronounces the words: "The gifts of God for the people of God." This is not only a statement—and an incredible one at that—but an invitation to accept God's gifts, to partake of them freely and with gratitude. This invitation to take Communion—to be nourished and fortified—is extended in churches daily around the world. Through our individual participation we renew our personal commitment to God. By coming to the communion table with others we bind ourselves to others who also seek to follow God's ways more closely.

Spiritual seekers today are rediscovering the power of ritual, the bodily reenactment of some aspect of our relationship with the holy. Communion, or the Eucharist as it is often called, has long been one of the central rites of the Christian faith because it speaks so powerfully and so mysteriously of our relationship with God. No matter how old we live to be or how often we partake in the act of communion, we will never fully grasp all the richness inherent in this sacred act, though our understanding of it deepens over time.

Communion is a gift of God for the people of God. The bread and the wine are given to all who come to the table regardless of worthiness. In the Roman Catholic and some Protestant traditions people are expected to go to confession—to cleanse themselves of sin—before taking communion. In most services of communion, regardless of denomination, a communal confession of sin and absolution occurs prior to the beginning of the service of Eucharist. Still, the gift of bread and wine—food for the journey—are ours, freely given by God. Communion, as the Rule of Taizé states, is given "to the sick of the People of God," to those who are "always weak and infirm"—in other words, to all of us.

Our response to this gift, as with all treasured gifts, is thankfulness. Even when we think we do not deserve what we receive, as a friend of mine often says, the proper liturgical response is "*thank you*." But the act of accepting communion also asks for an even deeper response from us. As part of the eucharistic service the minister reminds us that Jesus bid us to take the bread and the wine in remembrance of him. To take communion involves, then, remembering the life and death of Jesus and recommitting ourselves to modeling our lives on his example. We are given the bread and wine not only for our own healing, but as nourishment for the ongoing journey, to prepare us to go out into the world to help, support, and challenge others.

It is in this communal aspect of the Eucharist that much of its power lies. Communion is never a solitary act—it takes at least two people to celebrate or observe the Eucharist. We come together as a community of people of God to confess, to offer our thanks to God, and to commit ourselves—in the presence of God and one another—to being God's agents in a hurting world. This is not a private act, but a communal one that holds us accountable to all the members of our community, as well as God. Through Holy Communion we bind ourselves not only to God, but to the whole people of God, and we journey forth together.

Practice

Communion is best experienced when one is part of a worshipping community. In some churches, in fact, taking communion is considered a privilege of membership; the Roman Catholic Church permits only Catholics to take communion in their parishes. The largest majority of Protestant churches, however, ask only that a person be a baptized Christian before taking communion, though it is unlikely that anyone would ever check to see that this is actually the case. But it is through baptism that we join the Christian community— the whole Christian community, and not just our local church. When I travel, for instance, I take communion in congregations that are not my regular community, but do so with the sense that I am part of the whole Christian family. Still, the experience of communion deepens when one is a regular part of a community that celebrates this rite together. If you are not currently a part of a congregation, you might consider becoming part of one as a part of your experience of communion. As you participate in the eucharistic service try the following:

1. The actual rite (or ritual) is celebrated differently in the various denominations and congregations. Generally, however, there are introductory prayers that lead up to the actual distribution of the bread and wine. Use this time to listen contemplatively to the words of the prayers, to the story of Jesus' command to eat the bread and drink the wine. Without being overly analytical, just let the words be your guide. As you become more familiar with the service itself see what specific words speak to you at any given occasion. Even when the words are the same week after week, you may discover that some speak more clearly to you on one day than on another. Pay attention to the words that jump out at you and let those become part of your prayer.

2. The actual distribution of the bread and the wine usually happens in one of two ways—or a combination of both. Sometimes the bread and wine are brought to you in the pew, symbolizing that the gifts of God are brought freely to you, that you do not have to earn them. In other congregations, everyone comes forward to the altar and the bread and wine are given out there. This method reminds us of our own acceptance of God's gifts, which we have come to receive. Occasionally a congregation will distribute the bread and ask the parish to come forward for the cup, combining both theological approaches. Pay attention to the method of distribution of the

elements (the bread and the wine) and see what it means for them to be handed to you versus going forward to accept them.

3. After you have fed on the bread and wine take some time to reflect on what you have been given and what that gift demands, in return, from you. For what are you grateful? To what do you commit yourself now that you have been given the nourishment you need? What role can the church community play that will help you honor the commitments you are making?

Use Tension in Community Creatively

"We are also called to accept with compassion and humility the particular fragility, complexity, and incompleteness of each brother. Our diversity and our brokenness mean that tensions and friction are inevitably woven into the fabric of everyday life. They are not to be regarded as signs of failure. Christ uses them for our conversion as we grow in forbearance and learn to let go of the pride that drives us to control and reform our brothers on our own terms."
—The Rule of the Society of St. John the Evangelist

For me, thinking of tension as creative, rather than as a sign of failure, comes hard. My first instinct is to view difficult, stressful situations precisely as failures—the failure of someone else to act properly, think clearly, or do things the way I think they should be done. My own wish or need to control the environment and the people around me sometimes blinds me to the possibilities of diversity or of alternative ways of doing something, so I dig in my heels and try to push my own agenda. The older I get, however, the more I recognize that this type of response arises from my own brokenness. As I grow closer to God I am challenged to view tensions and friction as creative—as my teachers.

Most of us have no trouble learning from teachers. We enjoy learning from those who care about us and our progress, who enjoy watching us try and succeed at new things. We find it much more difficult, however, to learn from those whose teaching comes wrapped in some kind of unpalatable and bitter pill we must swallow. They behave in some way that annoys us or their beliefs appall us. They operate differently—either better or more poorly organized than we like. Or they communicate in ways we find cryptic. We might be able to avoid having one of these people as a close friend, but if we are members of any kind of community—church, work, social networks—sooner or later we will all encounter someone that we cannot avoid, someone from whom we can learn a great deal even under duress. But learning from these people will depend upon our willingness to do so.

Sometimes these people are those who have more professional knowledge than we do, some skill or talent that we need to learn. Other times they are people who are so similar to us that we find irritating in them the same qualities we dislike in ourselves. Maybe these people are just those who operate at a different pace, process information differently, or see through a different lens than us. They may come to the same conclusions we do via different paths, or they may arrive at a destination that seems completely foreign to us. No matter what the circumstances, these people are our teachers and they provide us with an opportunity "to grow in mutual forbearance and learn to let go of the pride that drives us to control and reform our brothers on our own terms." If we are to live well in community, if we are to grow in our relationship to God, we need to seek continually to remember that these people who challenge us so thoroughly are other beings beloved of God. Each of them is complex, frail, and incomplete, as is each of us.

One of the gifts of the community to each of us is these people who challenge us to practice compassion and humility. By accepting and even loving those we find difficult we may find it easier to accept our own shortcomings and ultimately love God more deeply. Or perhaps it is the reverse for you and you discover that as you love God more deeply it is easier to love yourself and even the most difficult of God's other creatures. For most of us, these two processes happen simultaneously. As we discover that God loves us unconditionally—warts and all—we find it possible to love (or at least accept) the warts on the person next to us. As we work to love the most difficult people in our churches, workplaces, or other communities, we find that the love we give others is actually love given to God. Each community of which we are a member, then, provides us with opportunities for spiritual growth and companionship; each brings us face-to-face with the wonder and diversity of God's creation.

Practice

1. Think of someone in one of your communities who irritates you.

2. If you can, be specific about the behaviors, attitudes, or practices that you find difficult and make a list of them. Many of us rehearse the list of things we dislike over and over in our minds. As you are writing

out your list, try to imagine that you are transferring your complaints from your thoughts to the paper and clear your mind as much as possible.

3. Looking over your list, try to think of ways in which some of the things you've written present you with opportunities to learn compassion, humility, or some other skill that God might be calling you to learn. Can you identify with some of the difficult behaviors because they exist within you as well? If a colleague's insecurity about an aspect of his or her life comes out as a strong desire to control others, for instance, can you use this knowledge to develop compassion for the other person's anxieties? (This does not imply that we allow others to harm us or others. But we may accomplish more in the situation if we can learn to respond out of compassion rather than anger, hatred, or self-righteousness.) Pray for the willingness and ability to make changes in your own perception and understanding.

4. Most of us will not be able to change our behavior or understanding of the person we dislike by doing this exercise once. Do it as often as needed.

5. Pray regularly to God for help in seeing this person as one of God's beloved. Ask God to show you what is special about the person who annoys you and confess your own inability to care for this person whenever you find yourself responding in a way that is less than compassionate and caring.

See a Spiritual Director

"The advice of a devout sage is a great asset . . . No matter how much you esteem your strength of will, place yourself under the direction of another."

—The Rule of Comgall

I f this rule were being written today it would most likely use different language. Perhaps it would read: Without a spiritual teacher (or companion or mentor) it is difficult to develop your spiritual life to its fullest extent. Trying to explore the depths of our relationship with God alone is akin to wandering in the forest solo. Even if you know your destination, you will find it hard to find your way without paths and markers on the journey. Seeing the path through thick clumps of tall trees proves difficult or impossible. You lose perspective, get lost, and maybe even discouraged. Sometimes, too, you just get bored and leave the forest entirely. Perhaps that is why increasingly large numbers of people today are turning to spiritual directors as guides. It was certainly what took me into spiritual direction many years ago, and what keeps me there now.

Spiritual direction is the process of two people (or sometimes a group) watching for God's presence in the life of the directee together. My first foray into spiritual direction ended less than satisfactorily because I expected the director to be my destination instead of a guide pointing toward God. I thought he would give me all the answers instead of pointing me along the path toward finding God's answers for me. (Patience has never been one of my greatest virtues.) By the time I found my second spiritual director, however, I was more willing to be pointed along the path instead of needing to arrive at the destination instantly. It was a difficult journey at times, focused on healing painful memories. That work, however, led me into closer relationship with God, as did the time spent with other directors since. Each director has taught me to see a different facet of God, one that I did not anticipate at the beginning of the director/directee relationship. One taught me about the healing power of God's love and the next taught me that God loved me unconditionally exactly as I was. My current one is helping me to learn to respond to the love of God by living out that knowledge in my daily activities.

Each director's style of guidance has been different; each has different questions or issues on which they focus. But they have all helped me see through the thick forest and look in the direction of the light. One did that by helping me remove the forest—the debris of my past—through a series of guided meditations. Others helped me move toward the light by continually asking how God might be at work in the daily activities and interactions of my life. Every director brings guidance based on his or her own experience and expertise, and when the fit is a good one between director and directee the journey toward the light of God can be exhilarating, exhausting, and deeply joy-filled.

Many books detail the practice of direction and provide basic information on what to expect from spiritual direction[29] so I will only mention a few of the details here. A spiritual director's task is to help you focus on your relationship with God, to help you discover the path along which God is leading you, and provide questions and suggestions that can further the journey. Many will talk with you about what goes on in your daily life and help you reflect on how God seems to be at work in your life at this particular time. The director may suggest some spiritual practices to you if they sense that you may be ready for a particular one or that something is well-suited to your needs at the moment.

They will also help you stay focused on your spiritual life. If you are at all like I am, my spiritual life can drop to the bottom of my to-do list when I am busy; knowing that I will see my spiritual director at regular intervals helps to prevent me from neglecting my relationship with God. A spiritual director will also, when needed, help you look at some of the hard truths of your life. A good director does this gently and nonjudgmentally, and their guidance in seeing both what you are doing to deepen and to avoid your relationship with God can be indispensable. At their best, they are companions, cheerleaders, friends, guides, and truth-tellers, and they are the people in your life who stand next to you pointing the way to God.

Practice

1. If you sense it might be helpful to enter into a spiritual direction relationship, think carefully about

what kind of director might be helpful. Do you want someone:

- with a background in a particular faith?
- who is/is not clergy?
- of a particular gender?
- within a particular geographic region?

2. It is important to have some sense of what you are looking for, though it is also helpful to remain open to other possibilities. You may also want to consider what you can afford to pay for spiritual direction. Most directors have a sliding scale for payment if money is a concern.

3. Though there are thousands of spiritual directors in this country and abroad, most of them are not listed in the Yellow Pages. Good places to inquire about directors include:

- clergy in local churches, particularly Catholic and Episcopal ones, though many mainline denominations are beginning to stress the value of spiritual direction and may be good sources of information
- a seminary, if you have a local one
- a monastery or convent
- a retreat center or spirituality institute

4. A good spiritual director recognizes that the fit between director and directee is essential to the relationship and expects to be interviewed. The director will want to form his/her own impression about the

viability of a relationship. Make appointments with one or more directors as an introductory interview and use that time to see if this is a person with whom you feel comfortable. Be prepared to say a little bit about what brings you to spiritual direction and what your hopes for the relationship might be. You might mention any particular questions or particular joys or concerns you want to bring before God in the spiritual direction relationship. If the fit between you and the director is a good one you will probably sense it. You can set up regular appointments at that point.

CHAPTER EIGHT

Care of Our Body

"So that we can better glorify God in our bodies each
of us shall take responsibility for maintaining his health
through regular exercise, hygiene, and prompt recourse
to medical attention . . ."
—The Rule of the Society of St. John the Evangelist

Skimming through ancient rules of life from various monastic communities, you may be hard-pressed to find
much focus on the body as a positive part of the spiritual
life. What you do find, more often than not, are the "do
nots" rather than "dos." The specific amount of food and
drink were specified in the ancient rules and not to be ex-
ceeded except, perhaps, on the church's feast days. Sleep was
sometimes limited by the demands of the daily prayer cycle.
Most rules had provisions for those who are ill or old, but
otherwise bodies were often considered a barrier to the soul's
perfection. Consequently, most ancient rules deal thoroughly
with prayer, study, worship, hospitality, and outreach, but
mention the body only in passing. There were exceptions to
this, certainly. Some early monastics recognized that excess

of any kind—deprivation or overindulgence—were harmful to the spiritual life and they created rules to deal with both extremes. But on the whole there seem to be far more negative images of the body in ancient literature than there are positive ones.

Contemporary rules have largely rectified this situation. We live in a more holistic culture today, one that sees the body as intimately connected and equal to the soul and the mind. We understand these three pieces operate as one and are unable to function separately. The body is no longer viewed as the enemy of the spiritual life, but as a valuable key to living it fully. If God is incarnate in the person of Jesus, then our bodies cannot be our enemies. Rather, as one writer says: "We are to learn to listen to the signals of our bodies, honoring them as one of the main ways God speaks to us and by which we can learn much unencountered truth about ourselves and our community."[30]

You may find it a new thought that God speaks to you through your body. If so, it may take some practice to begin learning to listen to what God is trying to tell you. We are far more accustomed to treating our bodies as simple instruments of our will. Ads, movies, and other media remind us regularly that our bodies are not perfect—that we are too short, too tall, too fat, and so on. We view illness as a betrayal by the body and do our best to ignore sickness whenever possible. We try to control our bodies, working them to death, without attention to the diet, rest, and exercise that help our bodies feel their best, allowing them to make positive contributions to our lives.

Learning to pay attention to our bodies and to give our physical needs the same attention we would give to prayer and outreach involves a degree of refocusing for many of us. But the payoff is that our bodies can provide us with valuable clues about our lives, our relationship to God and others, and to what is going on around us if we take the time to listen. Just as God speaks to us through prayer and study, God speaks to us through what is happening in our bodies. I had a spiritual director for several years who, during our conversations, would often ask me, "Where are you feeling that right now?" He taught me to recognize more fully my body's responses to stress, anger, and depression and to use those as clues to what God might be trying to tell me. He also taught me to pay attention to more open physical responses—feelings of relaxation or expansiveness—that were also clues to the path I could pursue. Several sections in this chapter suggest ways in which you, too, can begin to honor what is going on in your physical being.

Honoring our bodies and listening to what they may have to say to us is different, however, from freely indulging all of our physical desires without thought to the consequences. Touching whomever we wish however we wish, eating to excess, and other indulgences of the body do not contribute positively to our own body's needs, to the needs of others, or to our spiritual lives. These reflect selfish desires, rather than any concern about stewardship of the gift of our body. The rules in this chapter look at the balance we need to bring to the needs of our bodies if they are to serve us and God.

Listen to Your Body

"The hermit listens to his body, giving attention to health, exercise, work, proper diet, fasting and leisure. Because the Holy Trinity dwells within him, making him a 'Living House of Bread,' he nurtures and cares for the gift of his body and the sacredness of life."

—Hermits of Bethlehem

We often take poor care of the bodies God has given us. Bodies are somehow seen as inferior parts of our being, subject to the control of our minds. Ignoring how our bodies feel is not only an acceptable option in our culture, it is encouraged. Exercise is sometimes seen as something we do to control how our body feels, instead of something we do to help take care of ourselves. Pushing our bodies until they can no longer hold out is often seen as a sign of the strength of our character.

Perhaps instead of seeing our bodies as something we need to control or as something that occasionally controls us, we can begin to understand our bodies as an equal partner in our lives. Our bodies are actually an important source of information and wisdom for us. We learn and know many things through our senses rather than simply through thinking. We can learn to understand what is really going on in a meeting or conversation through the body language we observe in others or through the tone of voice we hear as much as through the words being said. Our experiences of cold, heat, and pain are important clues to physical well-being and safety. Taste and smell can tell us that food is rotten and not fit for us to consume.

Our bodies also give us important clues to how we are feeling physically, emotionally, and spiritually. As Flora Slosson Wuellner puts it, "Our body is not a minor but a major prophet!"[31] When confronted with a moral dilemma the knot in our stomach may help us know what God may be calling us to do. The headache we have all the time may be telling us that we have chosen a lifestyle that is not healthy. Our inability to sleep and the resulting exhaustion we feel deep in our bones may be telling us that change is in order. A sense of deep relaxation and peacefulness in our bodies helps us know that we have made a good decision or done something well. God speaks to us in physical ways, as much as in prayer or other activities. Listening to what our bodies are telling us is a way of listening to God.

For many years now I have had problems with back pain. The result primarily of too much heavy lifting for too many years, my back pain is also my clue to my general physical, emotional, and spiritual health. When I have overloaded my schedule or when I am under a lot of stress for too long a period of time, back pain builds. Inevitably when I am overly busy or stressed I fail to exercise properly or pray or sleep enough, which only aggravates the problem. I have, however, become so accustomed to back pain that I no longer tend to notice it until it is quite severe. When I go visit my massage therapist I find that the one painful spot that brought me to the massage table is only the tip of the iceberg. There are many layers of pain underneath that have been building up for some time. My body has been trying to tell me for many weeks that I am out of balance physically, emotionally, or spiritually and often all three at once. If I had taken the time to listen for God in the physical sensations of my life I might have avoided some of the extreme pain that comes from ignoring the more gentle pain. It is as if God has to holler at me some days before I am willing to listen.

The Hermits of Bethlehem, however, offer us a different way of life. By caring for our bodies—through exercise, work habits, diet, fasting, and rest—we acknowledge the gift of our bodies and care for them as we would any other valued present. Caring for our bodies is a way of acknowledging the sacredness of all of life, of acknowledging that God lives within us.

Practice

Most of us are poor stewards of our bodies at one time or another. Taking care of ourselves begins with a willingness to pay attention to what our bodies are telling us, to let them be messengers of God for us. If you are accustomed to paying very little attention to what your body is telling you it may take a little practice before you begin to listen to yourself regularly.

1. Begin by making a list of bodily reactions that you are aware of. Making a list will help you be conscious of what your body already knows. In what ways does your body let you know it is stressed?

Relaxed? Excited? Overly tired? Everyone has their own particular responses to emotional and spiritual stimuli, but common reactions to stress might include stomach knots or pain, backache, neck pain, and headache. Excitement might manifest itself in the sensation of limitless energy. Heavy fatigue might be visible in the face (dullness in the eyes, bags under the eyes) as well as in slumped posture, sore muscles, or in a total lack of energy. Relaxation may be accompanied by the cessation of many of the bodily reactions listed above, as well as increased body temperature and a sense of well-being.

2. Once you are aware of some of the tools your body uses to communicate with you, begin trying to notice when these various sensations occur. Watch for additional ways in which your body tells you what is going on and add them to your list. Chart the various things you notice about your reactions for two or three weeks.

3. Using the list of ways your body reacts, look for a balance between symptoms that indicate stress and those that allow your body to relax. Is your body telling you during ninety percent of the day that you are stressed? A certain amount of stress and excitement can be creative and energizing, but too much can be harmful to your well-being. If your body is in pain and discomfort a large part of most days, perhaps it is worth reevaluating the activities that seem to induce those feelings. Pain, of course, may be related to a chronic medical condition over which you may have little control, but some chronic pain

does respond very well to attention paid in the form of exercise or relaxation.

The point of this exercise is to become aware of what your body is telling you. It may be hollering for exercise of a particular sort, for more rest, for a better diet, or for less stressful living conditions. Becoming aware of what your body is telling you is the first step toward making changes that lead to healthier and more sacred living.

Sleep Enough

"For our feeble flesh could not possibly be defrauded
of the whole night's rest and yet keep its vigour un-
shaken throughout the following day without sleepiness
of mind and heaviness of spirit . . ."
— The Twelve Books of John Cassian on the
Institutes of Coenobia

Even if you haven't raised a child you've probably witnessed this scenario: A normally delightful child has
turned into a monster. The child is whining and cranky, argues, cries, and makes demands until the child's parent is at
his or her wit's end. Everyone around the scene is thinking
the same thing: This kid needs a nap.

And who among us has not felt like that overly tired child
some days? We may have learned to control our response to
fatigue, but at heart most of us feel whiney and cranky and
ready to be at rest. Lost in a sea of to-do lists, however, we
often rise early and go to bed late. For many of us, as well,
our first real chance to think about the day comes the mo-

ment we put our head upon the pillow; we stay awake for hours processing the day's events. Is it any wonder that we are often tired?

Getting enough rest is actually an important part of our spiritual life; without enough rest we may have inadequate resources to practice the rest of our rule. I learned this years ago, when I was a lot younger and could handle sleep deprivation much better than I can today. Every summer I went on a ten-day trip with about eight other adults and around twenty-five high school teenagers. For ten days we worked and played together, but we did a lot less sleeping than the adults might have liked. Among twenty-five teens, there are always a few (and they vary from night to night) who can stay up until all hours. I thoroughly enjoyed the trips, but I was always very tired when I got home, and usually long before that. Being present to the group, listening well, and tolerating teenage antics got more difficult as the ten days progressed. Without adequate sleep I did not feel as well grounded, as connected to God, and my well of inner resources ran dangerously low.

Most of us don't deprive ourselves of sleep at this level on a regular basis, but many of us do sleep less than we need to. Ideally, we should be able to wake up on our own each morning, feeling refreshed. If your alarm clock is waking you out of a deep sleep every morning, you are probably not getting enough rest. We tend to treat sleep as an interruption to our lives, as a necessary evil that we tolerate. We wish that we could make our bodies do without sleep. But we have been given bodies and bodies need rest. Often they need more rest than many of us allow ourselves.

Maybe it is helpful to remember that sleep is actually a gift from God. The Book of Common Prayer's translation of Psalm 127:2 tells us: "It is in vain that you rise so early and go to bed so late; vain, too, to eat the bread of toil, for he gives to his beloved sleep." These words, written centuries ago, are just as true now as they were then. Perhaps we are actually being vain when we deprive our bodies of sleep. We are playing God by trying to control things that are beyond our grasp. More than that, we are refusing to accept one of God's gifts to us: the gift of sleep.

Practice

How much sleep each of us needs varies enormously. Experts claim that we need about seven to eight hours of sleep a night, but you may need only six or as much as nine or ten hours of sleep a night. How much you need will vary with age, and even with the circumstances of your life. During periods of high stress you may need more sleep than you would under less difficult circumstances. You may need to experiment with your body's requirements before you find the amount of sleep you need before waking on your own, refreshed and ready for another day. If you currently get less than eight hours of sleep a night, and you feel tired, try sleeping a full eight hours every night for a week and see if that helps you to feel more alert. Add or subtract hours from that schedule as needed.

If you are having trouble getting to sleep, or regulating your body's need for sleep, try some of the following suggestions:

1. Our bodies have a noticeable natural rhythm of their own if we pay attention. You may have a sense that you are a "morning person" or a "night person" already; this relates to your body's own clock. Insofar as you are able, adjust your schedule to allow

your body to sleep and work in a rhythm that matches your own. You may find, for instance, that you need less sleep if you are a night person and you do not try to force your body to go to bed at 10:00 P.M. and rise at 6:00 A.M.

2. If you are like many of us and you wait to process the day's events until bedtime, you will be losing valuable sleep time. Even if you are in bed for a full eight hours, you may be spending one or two of those reviewing the day. Try to find a time earlier in the evening to sit and quietly think about the day, instead of waiting until your head hits the pillow. Writing in a journal about the day, talking to someone, or any other method that helps you process the day may help prevent you from doing it when you want to be sleeping. By doing this, you might also discover that you are just trying to do too much many days, and that a less stressful schedule will improve your ability to sleep.

3. Foods and health supplements can help you sleep when you find it difficult to rest. Vitamin supplements, as well as various herbal remedies available in health food stores, may help you get to sleep more easily. A physician or homeopath may be able to help you select the proper supplement.

4. Many of us have trouble sleeping because we do not get enough exercise. Lots of physical exertion right before bed, however, tends to keep us awake. If you regularly have trouble sleeping, see if you can work even fifteen minutes of walking or another type of exercise into your schedule most days.

5. A period of relaxation exercise or prayer may also help with sleep, though some find that extended prayer right before bed can actually disrupt their rest. But taking time early in the evening for meditation or prayer can help you to reduce the anxieties or concerns that may be keeping you awake.

Whether you have trouble sleeping or not, you might find it helpful to dedicate your sleep to God each evening. Along with brushing your teeth and whatever else you do at bedtime, you might establish a brief ritual that acknowledges the gift of sleep and turns the day's events over to God before retiring. One of my own favorite evening prayers comes from the Episcopal Book of Common Prayer; this prayer has soothed me to sleep many a night.

"Keep watch, dear Lord, with those who work, or watch, or weep this night, and give your angels charge over those who sleep. Tend the sick, Lord Christ; give rest to the weary, bless the dying, soothe the suffering, pity the afflicted, shield the joyous; and all for your love's sake. Amen."
—The Book of Common Prayer, 124

Express Affection

"We express our regard for one another not only in words, but in gestures which give our bodies a part to play in the interchange of affection, as is natural for men who believe wholeheartedly in the incarnation. We are free to cheer one another with open arms of welcome and to show our care and sensitivity through touch."
—The Rule of the Society of St. John the Evangelist

Some years ago a friend of mine worked in a pediatric ward caring for very sick newborns who were likely to spend many of their first months of life in a hospital room. Oftentimes when I would visit her I would see candy stripers, nurses aides, and others simply holding and rocking the babies. Those infants needed touch as much as they needed medicine if they were to become healthy and thrive. Being held, rocked, and talked to or sung to was a powerful part of their care.

Through our growing years and into adulthood that need

for touch we all have as infants remains strong. There is something deeply instinctual about our need to know, give, and receive affection. When we are in love we long to have our lover's arms around us. When we are sad we need a hug. Something done well is rewarded with a pat on the shoulder. Anxiety can be relieved by having someone hold our hand. Our blood pressure can even be lowered by petting a dog or cat. Something about the physicality of touch seems to validate our very being and the emotions we are experiencing. Touching can also be deep communication, sometimes saying much more than words can express.

Touch has also gotten a lot of people in trouble in recent years. Inappropriate touch, often associated with sex or sexual harassment, has made news headlines locally and nationally. In the office, in our churches, and in social situations physical contact has been used by those who have power over those in less powerful positions. The rules on when, where, and how to express ourselves physically have not necessarily changed, but hopefully our sensitivity to inappropriate contact has increased.

Inappropriate contact aside, we are physical people who need to touch and be touched by others. This is reflected even in the biblical texts. In the Gospels, Jesus often reached out to help and bless people through touch. When people brought him children to bless he wrapped his arms around them. Jesus healed a leper simply by touching him. And when a woman who had been hemorrhaging for twelve years needed help she reached out and touched Jesus' cloak and she was healed. Jesus received healing by being touched as well. At dinner one evening in the home of Simon the Pharisee, Jesus was approached by a woman who bathed his feet with her tears and dried them with her hair. Simon was outraged, but this woman had performed a kindness that should have been performed by Simon as the host. Jesus received her gift and blessed her.

Touch for us, just as for Jesus, is a way of healing and being healed. Some years ago I worked as a hospice volunteer. One day I was called to a home by a couple who needed to go out for a while. They needed me to stay with the wife's mother who was very old and very close to death. The mother was barely eating and was delusional most of the time. Restricted by frailty to her bed, she had reverted to speaking German, the language of her childhood, and she lived in the past. Being new at hospice work I was terrified when this woman got very agitated and began to speak a language I did not understand. I could find nothing to do for her except to hold her hand and stroke her arm. Much to my surprise the touch seemed to quiet and relax her; she soon drifted off into a quiet sleep. The touch reassured her and it did so in ways that were deeper than any words I could have uttered.

In many respects people in today's culture, perhaps hyperaware of all the inappropriate uses of physical contact, have lost the willingness and ability to express affection bodily. We have been taught that it is fine for lovers to touch each another, but unless we are with our lover we do not walk down the street holding hands with someone. Somewhere around the junior high school years we decided that we don't want to be hugged by our parents anymore. We seem to lose track of most other bodily contact as well, unless it relates to sexual activity. But by giving up our willingness to touch and be touched, we have lost the opportunity to "show our care and sensitivity" and to experience the caring touch of someone else. We have lost an important source of comfort, caring, and healing for ourselves and for those for whom we care.

Practice

If you find it difficult to hug people or to express any affection physically, think back to your own family of origin's practices regarding touch.

1. Who hugged you when you were a child? Was there a time that they stopped hugging you, and if so, who instigated that, and why? Did playing with friends as a child involve any physical contact? Was that encouraged or discouraged by the adults around you? What kinds of touch were labeled appropriate and inappropriate for you as a child? Was punishment meted out in physical ways? How does this color your ideas about touch now? Were you the object of inappropriate contact of any kind?

2. If you suffered physical or sexual abuse as a child, touch may be very difficult for you and it may be very helpful to get some professional assistance in dealing with the impact these incidents have on your life. If you simply grew up in a family in which physical contact was discouraged or just not offered you might begin carefully to explore what touch can add to your life. A simple way to begin experiencing the power of touch is to get a massage from a certified massage therapist. A massage is a wonderful way, in a safe environment, to begin to experience the relaxation and rejuvenation of touch. You will probably find that it not only relaxes sore muscles but leaves you feeling emotionally and perhaps spiritually peaceful as well.

3. As you begin to feel more comfortable with touch you may discover that your friends enjoy a hug, that you have been the one giving the signal a hug is not appropriate. We can do this rather clearly by sticking out a hand for a handshake when we meet people or more subtly by backing up so that others know we do not wish to be hugged. If you are ready to let others hug you, begin by avoiding both of the behaviors above and hugs may come your way quite naturally. As you feel ready, begin hugging those who are close to you. If you are in doubt about whether or not a hug is okay, ask if you can give someone a hug. It may feel awkward to initiate a hug in the beginning, but you are likely to find it becomes quite comfortable before long.

Rest When You Are Ill

"... [N]or shall you sit idle ... but with a quick hand
you shall prepare ropes for the warps of mats, although
exception is made for the infirmity of the body to which
leave must be given for rest."
— The Rule of Pachomius

Commercial after commercial on television, particularly
during the winter cold and flu season, touts medicines
that can help us feel perfectly well, even if we are very ill.
They claim they can ease the sore throat, cure the congestion,
reduce the fever, and generally make it possible for us to
continue working as if our body were not sick at all. We can
make that all-important presentation after all; the account
will be secured. In today's world we don't have time for illness. That attitude is reinforced by a health care system that
focuses on reducing hospital stays to the shortest possible
time, forcing people to complete their recovery elsewhere.

Some of our attitudes about illness are influenced by our
approach to work. In a world that often feels beyond our

control, work generally feels like something we can make happen according to our specifications. We cannot prevent ourselves from catching germs or from coming down with diseases that make life difficult, but sometimes we ignore our illnesses and continue working. We try to take control of our bodies, instead of letting our bodies control us. Not allowing our bodies to rest when they are ill is a way of thumbing our nose at God, of pretending that we are indispensable rather than just one more of God's creatures.

Being very ill and succumbing to sickness is also often connected to feelings of shame and incompetence somehow. We seem to believe that if we are ill we must have done something wrong to bring on the infirmity. This sense that we bring all sickness upon ourselves is an ancient one. When Job suffers unspeakable losses and physical hardships in the Old Testament his friends confront him and ask what he did to anger God so deeply. To think that someone else is sick because they did not do something correctly helps us feel more invulnerable to illness. We blame the victim and believe that if we do everything right, we will not develop cancer or some other illness. God's answer to this, however, is a stern one. We cannot know why illness strikes us, any more than we can understand the complete workings of the universe. We are assured, however, that illness is not a sign of moral weakness or ineptitude. We are also told that God weeps with us when we are ill. Illness is not a punishment from a vengeful God who takes satisfaction in our suffering.

Consequently, many of the ancient and contemporary rules make provision for illness, age, and infirmity of various sorts. Pachomius's monasteries in the fourth century made ample provision for illness, advising rest when the body is sick. Benedict and others made similar provisions in their rules. The tradition of nurturing the body when ill remains strong in monasteries even today, as stated in The Rule of the Society of St. John the Evangelist: "So that we can better glorify God in our bodies each of us shall take responsibility for maintaining his health through regular exercise, hygiene, and prompt recourse to medical attention as soon as he becomes aware of any significant symptom."[32] Care is taken to help the body stay healthy, says The Rule of the Society of St. John the Evangelist, but bodies sometimes get sick anyway, and they should be cared for when ill just as they are when they are well.

Some illnesses are so severe they force us to stop and rest. Sometimes these health problems are chronic or life-threatening and we have little choice but to pay attention. Many of us with the common cold or flu, however, continue to go to work, making ourselves miserable and sharing the germs with our colleagues who will be miserable, too.

Instead of trying to ignore our health problems perhaps we can use them instead as sabbaths for our bodies and souls. These are times to make self-care a priority. We can listen to our body's limits, honor them, and give ourselves the rest and nourishment we need to feel better. We can also allow ourselves to be taken care of, giving others an opportunity to minister to us. By not spreading our germs around and martyring ourselves to the gods of work or whatever else makes us feel important, we are respecting our bodies within which God dwells and equipping ourselves and others better for ministry in the world.

Practice

Following a rule about resting when you are ill may require that you look at your own perhaps unconscious attitudes toward sickness and your role in the world. Some of the following questions may help you uncover valuable information that will help you change how you approach being sick.

1. Think about your own attitudes toward being sick. How were illnesses handled when you were a child? Did someone take care of you when you were sick? What did they do for you? How did it make you feel? Do your childhood experiences of being sick influence how you handle being ill today?

2. What influences the way you deal with illness and rest today? Does being sick make you angry at your body, as if you have been betrayed? What other attitudes and experiences might prevent you from resting and caring for yourself or allowing yourself to be cared for when you are sick?

3. If you had a sick child to care for, how would you do that? How would you want that child to feel? What prevents you from allowing yourself the same level of care?

4. If you were to miss a day of work or chores due to the onset of a cold or flu, what would happen? Sometimes we simply must work sick when we are able, but many times we can call on others for help with our tasks or let the tasks wait for a day or two. The next time you are ill see if you can discern whether or not it is really necessary for you to work or if you can stop even for a half day and rest.

Wear Something to Remind You of Your Rule

"A simple reception service takes place when the application procedure is completed, during which a medal is presented to the new Associate. The medal should be worn openly, if possible."

—The Rules for Associates of the Community of the Holy Spirit

In the past, and sometimes still today, monks and nuns wear habits—robes specified by the monastic order. These habits prevented monks and nuns from using clothing to glorify themselves; a simple habit worn by all reminded everyone that all were equal in the sight of God. Habits also served to remind the religious of their ties to the church and to God. They were, and are, a visible sign of one's commitment to loving God and to a particular monastic community.

The robes or habits worn in monasteries are also accompanied by other items of clothing or accessories. Ropes tied around the waist, hoods, pectoral crosses, and rings are part of various monastic uniforms. Each piece of the outfit is intended to remind the monk or nun of some aspect of their membership in the community and their commitments. John Cassian for instance, recommends that monks don "very small hoods coming down to the end of the neck and shoulders, which only cover the head, in order that they constantly be moved to preserve the simplicity and innocence of little children by imitating their actual dress."[33] Likewise, the cords worn around the waists of the contemporary monks of The Society of St. John the Evangelist are "an ancient sign of readiness that can summon us to be prepared to meet Christ whenever he should come. The knots tied in the cord at profession [the taking of vows] are signs to the hand and eye of the vows we have made to abide faithfully until he comes."[34]

One of the ways, then, that we can help ourselves remember to keep God at the center of our lives is to wear something that is a constant reminder. What that item needs to be is a matter of personal taste. Perhaps it is a cross on a chain, or a ring or pin with a Celtic or some other significant design. Medals in honor of various saints are also worn by those who find a role model in a particular saint. Even a simple friendship bracelet made of string, if it reminds you of your relationship with God, is fine. It does not matter what item you choose to wear, as long as it helps you remember God's presence in your life and your commitment to your rule.

Whether or not you wear the item in a conspicuous place is also a matter of choice. John Cassian suggested that monks avoid wearing inadequate habits since that would lead to pride in one's humility. Others, such as the Community of the Holy Spirit quoted above, suggest that Associates (laypeople who choose to affiliate with the order) wear their medals in a place where they can be seen. Perhaps you will choose to wear an item only at specific times—during your prayer time, for instance. Choose whatever works best for you. Wearing something next to your skin that may be invisible to others is just as good as wearing an item that others can see and comment upon. Having it on all the time is as good as intentionally putting it on for prayer or other times of devotion. The goal is to wear an item in such a way that it reminds you of God's presence in your life.

Practice

1. It is important to choose carefully the item that you wish to wear. Spend some time thinking about what kind of symbol might be meaningful to you. Some possibilities were mentioned above, but there are many others. A beautiful stone or other natural object that reminds you of the bounty of God's creation may also be meaningful. Or perhaps a shell,—like those that were given to some pilgrims on their sacred journeys—would be useful.

2. Take some time, as well, in finding not only the right object, but one that appeals to you either aesthetically or for a particular emotional or spiritual reason. If, for instance, you choose to wear a small cross on a chain, take the time to locate one that seems to have been made just for you.

3. Once you have selected what you will wear, before you put it on offer a prayer of thanks for the awareness that it will help to bring into your life. Ask God

to bless the item and use it to remind you of your rule and of God's loving presence in your life. Place the item on your body and give thanks to God for this new reminder.

Exercise for the Good of Your Soul

"For practicing equally the virtues of the body and of
the soul, they balance what is due to the outer man;
steadying the slippery motions of the heart and the shift-
ing fluctuations of the thoughts by the weight of labour . . ."

—The Twelve Books of John Cassian on the
Institutes of the Coenobia

I am never more aware of the connection between exercise
and my spiritual and emotional health than during the
darker winter months. The lack of sunshine sometimes makes
me blue. Once I am a little bit depressed I stop exercising
and not long after I stop exercising I stop praying. All of
which makes me even more depressed. It is often by dragging
myself off to the gym that I can begin to short-circuit this
miserable circle. Once I begin exercising I begin to feel more
energetic and lively and that translates into the ability to pray
again. The inner and outer parts of me are deeply connected;
I ignore one at the peril of the other.

Exercise or physical activity, then, is a spiritual discipline, one that connects the body, soul, and mind. It is something I do not only to keep my body feeling healthy, but it energizes, calms, and frees my emotions and my spirit as well. If, for instance, we are very stressed or angry our bodies often respond with tightness while our emotions seem beyond control. Intense physical exercise can release both the strain in the muscles and the emotional gridlock we feel. When I am anxious or frustrated I often find that taking a brisk walk—even a short fifteen-minute one—releases enough strain that I can relax and begin to consider new options or solutions. Trying to engage in the practice of contemplative prayer is almost always futile when my body has been captured by some strain. Exercise—movement—is what allows me to be grounded again. My body, emotions, and spirit relax and begin to feel expansive instead of constricted. Exercise is, indeed, a spiritual discipline.

Or, as friends of mine would say, "Grace is physical."[35] Phil Porter and Cynthia Winton-Henry lead workshops on what they call InterPlay. These workshops help people learn to play again—to be creative with their bodies while noticing the effects on their emotional and spiritual life. Phil and Cynthia teach people to recognize body responses that are the opposite of stress. These open, relaxed, and expansive sensations—often brought on by physical exertion—are what Porter calls "the physicality of grace." Whereas stress takes a toll on our bodies, "grace has long-term positive physical effects."[36]

During a one-week workshop I took from Phil and Cynthia I was surprised to find just how strong the connection between body and soul was. The workshop challenged me to the core, not physically, but emotionally and spiritually. The activities themselves were not hard or complex or even physically taxing. But learning to express myself bodily—to let my body convey something of who I am in movement and in physical contact with others—was difficult at first. By uncrossing my arms and legs, by leaving behind my safe postures and attitudes, instead letting my body move freely and energetically, I ended up discovering a great deal about myself. My fears, my hopes, and my wishes were open to me in completely new ways that week. As this happened for others in the workshop we all began, in our new vulnerability, to sense the presence of grace, of God within everyone in the room. We were learning that bodies are a gift from God and need expression whether through play or exercise. Letting them speak, and listening to their wisdom, is a way of listening to God.

Practice

1. The key to enjoying exercise is finding something to do that you enjoy and that helps you feel relaxed and energized. Find something realistic for you, that you know you can continue doing. Walking is one very basic exercise that is helpful to most people. A twenty-minute walk three times a week can give you time to think and clear your mind, to observe the world around you while it rejuvenates your body. Working the walk into a lunch hour can be especially helpful during a busy or stressful day. I am particularly fond of going for a walk at the end of the workday, as it helps me to clear my mind of work and enjoy my evening.

2. There are a variety of other forms of exercise you might find enjoyable as well: yoga, jogging, aerobics,

tai chi, weight lifting, team sports of various kinds. If you are finding it difficult to work exercise into your rule, try joining a gym or a class of some sort. Sometimes the financial investment you make in joining one of these encourages you to keep going. You might also consider finding an exercise partner, someone who has a schedule that is similar to yours and is willing to commit to exercising with you regularly. A preset or regular appointment with an exercise partner can be just the motivation you need. Hiring a personal trainer can accomplish the same thing.

3. How much exercise you need and of what sort is the subject of debate among experts. Some say three periods of twenty minutes each is adequate, while others say that short periods of exercise five to six times a week is more beneficial. Listen to your own body's wisdom about what seems to help you feel better physically, emotionally, and spiritually. Find a type of exercise that fits your body's ability—something that challenges you but not so much that you end up hurt or miserable. Or choose a combination of exercises that you enjoy. Maybe there are things you can do in the summer that you can't do in winter or vice versa. Vary your exercise program to keep it fresh and interesting. Whatever you choose, however, should provide emotional and spiritual benefits as well as physical ones. Grace is what happens when your body is relaxed and energetic. Find a routine that brings more grace, not less, into your life.

Eat Properly

"Some are of the opinion that to eat small meals frequently is more proper and more salutary for the soul than to eat large meals at irregular intervals."

—Rule of the Céli Dé

I don't know about you, but I can get bogged down with some pretty poor eating habits, especially when I am busy. I skip breakfast, grab half a sandwich for lunch as I continue to work, and usually stuff something sweet down my throat in the mid or late afternoon because I am starving but too busy to eat properly. Then after work I eat a huge dinner and often a large snack before bedtime. The near-fasting during the day, supplemented by coffee and sweets, saps all the energy reserves from my body. Then I fill myself to excess in the evening and find myself too sleepy afterward to want to do anything interesting. Not only is this poor for my body's health, but it usually disrupts my spiritual life as well. Especially when the schedule is very heavy, I can find myself as oblivious to God during my day as I am to my own body's needs. And in the evening, stuffed from overeating, I am too sleepy to pray or read or even think about God's presence in my life that day.

That's my set of bad habits around food, but you may have others. Many of us go too long without eating during a day and then fill ourselves with poor quality or fast food when we have a moment. Furthermore, we often eat on the go, begrudging the few moments it takes us to wolf down some food. Even the five minutes it takes to heat something in the microwave feels like forever. Or we eat while continuing to work or while doing some other activity, which prevents us from even enjoying the food we are ingesting. Having to feed our bodies has become yet another chore, a nuisance activity that we try to do as few times or with as little thought as possible during the day.

Our lack of attention to the food we eat sometimes comes from paying homage to the gods of work or busy-ness, the false idols we substitute for God. We put our needs for success in the work world ahead of our own physical needs and claim that we simply don't have time to shop, cook, prepare food, or take a lunch break. Eating poorly, then, can be a sort of spiritual arrogance. We reject the gift of our bodies by neglecting to care for them adequately.

Some of us eat poorly by continually dieting in order to attain the "perfect body." Rather than developing a healthy diet, we starve ourselves. Then when we can stand it no longer, we eat everything in sight. Eating poorly and the eating disorders that sometimes accompany the desperate search for perfection are often signs that our emotional and spiritual health are suffering as much as, or more than, our bodies.

Nutritionists and doctors have long told us that eating smaller quantities of healthy food more regularly through the day promotes better health. By eating a meal more frequently than once or twice a day we tend to eat smaller amounts of food at one sitting, since we are not completely famished. We also make it more feasible to eat the variety of foods we need in order to stay as healthy as possible. Eating four or five servings of fruit and vegetables daily, for instance, if one only eats once or twice a day, becomes quite difficult. Eating often, and in smaller quantities, keeps our energy levels more even, and this helps to keep us more balanced emotionally and spiritually. Think of it as you would a fireplace: If you let the logs on the fire burn down to embers it is much harder to restart the fire than if you feed it a small amount of logs more often. The fire fed continuously burns more consistently and keeps us warm. In the same manner, feeding ourselves regularly allows our energy levels to be more consistent, which allows our emotional and spiritual energies to stay more balanced. This, in turn, helps us to pay more attention to those around us, to respond to others out of love and compassion and not from the caffeine and sugar jitters.

Practice

Finding the time to eat well can be challenging, especially when we lead busy lives. Many of us eat out often simply to avoid the time it takes to shop, cook, and clean up. But eating out all the time can also mean that we eat the wrong kinds of foods and too much of them. Or we stop in the grocery store every night on the way home from work and, feeling famished by this time, we buy all the wrong kinds of foods. Instead we need to find simple ways to have healthy and nutritious foods handy when we need them. One way to do that is to plan the week's menus in advance and then go shopping just once for the week's food. You may be surprised how much less time this takes than trying to figure out what to eat meal by meal and shopping multiple times during the week.

1. Try to find a half hour during the week to think about what you would like to eat during the coming week. (This has the added benefit of really helping you learn about what you are actually eating now, which can be a sobering experience.) Try to come up with menus for at least three meals a day: breakfast, lunch, and dinner. This does not mean that you need to plan to cook for all these meals or even that you will prepare all meals. If you enjoy eating out, plan that some of your meals will be restaurant ones. But think ahead a little and make a list of foods that you want to have available during the coming week. Think about making some dishes for dinner that make good leftovers for lunch the next day as a way of saving some time on cooking. Or plan to make a large pan of something with the intention of freezing individual portions for future use when you are strapped for time.

2. While you are planning meals, think about a couple of snacks for each day. For some this will mean a morning and afternoon snack, while others will find that an afternoon and evening snack works best. Make them healthy snacks—fresh fruits or vegetables, cheese and crackers, yogurt, a bagel, or other foods that provide some nutritional value and energy.

3. Go shopping for all foods you will need for the week.

4. Post your menus on the refrigerator to remind your-self of your food plan for the week. If you work away from home, this will also help you to remember what you've planned for lunch and what snacks you might take with you to work.

5. If you won't have much time to cook during the week, cook a large meal or casserole on Sunday and eat the leftovers on weeknights.

One of the side benefits of shopping and eating this way is that we often end up buying only the amount of food we really need and wasting less. In the process of feeding ourselves properly, and tending to God's temple, we also become better stewards of the earth's food resources.

CHAPTER NINE

Reaching Out

"The one who falls sick shall be led by the master to the refectory for the sick. And if he needs a mantle or a tunic or anything else . . . let the master himself get these from the ministers and give them to the sick brother."

—The Rule of Pachomius

The preceding chapters in part two of this book have been about care of your own spiritual life, and while this chapter and the one that follows also focus on your life with God, they look at your relationship with others rather than your personal relationship with God. When God is the center of our lives, when we know that we are God's beloved, we have the obligation and the great joy of sharing that treasure with others. The Jerusalem Community Rule of Life states this very simply and beautifully: "In your heart God has excavated an immense space where he has placed a precious treasure. From now on you have the twofold duty of receiving and giving: sharing the treasure of the kingdom you bear within you and stretching the area of your tent for those around you."[37]

All that we have looked at so far—our prayer lives, our search for God, our time in spiritual community and study, and even taking care of our bodies—allows God to excavate a huge space within us. That introspection is a necessary prerequisite to reaching out to others, but it is not the goal of the journey. Philip Newell, a wonderful Anglican spiritual writer, puts it this way: "To be unaware of what is within us, or to be neglectful of it, will be to undermine our own attempts at loving others. If we are not alert to the Self who is within our self and all selves, what will the extent of our self-giving be? . . . [I]n giving time and attention to such awareness we will grow in our understanding of the sacredness that is in others."[38] In other words, our prayer time, the time we spend in spiritual community and in study, is not meant simply for our own pleasure and satisfaction. It brings us alive to God's presence not only in ourselves but in everything and everyone around us. When we are conscious of the gift of God's presence within us, we begin to see through God's eyes and respond, as God would, to the pain and injustice in the world around us. We share the love God has given each of us with others who are in need, because we cannot help doing so.

When we live with God at the center of our lives we share not only God's love with others, but all our resources as well. All that we have, ultimately, is a gift from God, and it seems quite reasonable to return the money, time, and talents that we have on loan. Each of us, however, gives differently, according to our own abilities and understandings. Some are able to give a great deal of money, while others give of their time; some of us can even give both. There are large public gifts such as those of some philanthropists, while others, like the widow in Luke, give only a few coins. But both types of gifts are great ones, because each gives what he or she can. There are people in the world who have the gift of fighting for justice—people like Dr. Martin Luther King, Jr., who fought for the civil rights of all citizens. Others serve in less visible capacities, feeding the homeless in soup kitchens day after day. Ultimately, the method by which we reach out to others does not matter to God. God only cares that we share the gifts we have been given in whatever ways we can each manage.

A life focused on God leads us into service. Like the master with the sick brother in the rule above, we must—each of us—help the one less fortunate and take responsibility for providing what our sick brother needs. We must be the presence of God for those less fortunate than ourselves and respond in love, giving from the resources that we have on loan.

Simplify Your Needs

"Trusting in the Father, Christ chose for himself and his mother a poor and humble life, even though he valued created things attentively and lovingly. Let the Secular Franciscans seek a proper spirit of detachment from temporal goods by simplifying their own material needs."

—The Rule of the Secular Franciscans

A few years ago I decided to take a job that entailed a move of about three thousand miles. That, in turn, meant packing all the things I owned and I quickly discovered that my closets, bookshelves, and cupboards were full of things I hadn't used in years. There were boxes of clothes I had outgrown, books I would never read again, knicknacks and all sorts of other things that I hadn't even unpacked from the move I'd made five years prior. So while I packed over the following two months I got rid of the things I hadn't used in years and would not be likely to use again. I gave boxes of clothes, dishes, and household items away to a secondhand store that used the income to help the poor. I took boxes of books to the local public library to sell at their annual library sale or put on their shelves as they chose. I tried to take as little across the country with me as possible. Two years after that move I moved to another new home and went through the process again, getting rid of things I hadn't used in the intervening two years. Without a doubt I still have too many things in my home that I don't need, but there are many fewer than there were two years ago.

Most monastic rules require men and women who enter their orders to give away all or almost all of what they own. We have somewhat romantic notions of what that means today, but the reality was often quite different. Men and women who entered monastic life, for instance, often gave their worldly goods to their monastic community, which was frequently housed in spacious dwellings. As one historian writes, ". . . [T]he poverty of the individual, living in a spacious and wealthy institution tended to be psychological rather than material."[39] As early as the sixth century, then, and perhaps earlier, monks and nuns struggled with the proper attitude toward material goods and were asked to hold what they had lightly, in a poverty of spirit, even while they were often surrounded by plenty.

Although we live with more material goods than do monks and nuns, we struggle with the same paradox today. The various rules do not ask us to live on the streets, deprived of all worldly goods. But many of them, like the one above, do suggest that we practice a "proper spirit of detachment from temporal goods," valuing what we have but not making it—rather than God—the center of our world. In the midst of a consumer culture that encourages shopping and material possessions as the cure for almost anything that ails us, this rule suggests that we simplify our needs and surround ourselves with only those things that are truly important. This kind of "voluntary simplicity," as it is often called today, can help us to reprioritize our lives and make space for God.[40]

Practicing voluntary simplicity also allows many of us to escape the endless loop of consumerism. We work hard to earn the money to buy more things, but acquisition tends to lead to a desire for even more, so we work harder to pay for more new stuff. Many of us purchased all those items on a credit card and we find ourselves in all sorts of debt, which leads to more anxiety and the need to work even harder. In our consumer society money and possessions easily become the center of our world, rather than God. And even if we think of God occasionally, we are working so hard that we don't have time to give God (and often friends and family) more than a passing thought. "No one can serve two masters," Jesus says in Matthew 6:24, "for a slave will either hate the one and love the other, or be devoted to the one and despise the other. You cannot serve God and wealth." God can be the center of our world, or possessions can take that place, but there is only one center.

When our possessions and the need for more of them rules our lives we also begin to believe that all we own comes purely from our own hard work and that no one else has a right to what is ours. We forget that what we have around us came to us, in large part, because of the gifts and skills God gave us. We are in God's debt. I remember that many people bought me lunches and dinners while I was in college and couldn't afford meals in restaurants very easily. When I was out of school and employed I bought the meals for others who needed the help as a way of repaying the universe. We cannot always repay the one who helped us. There is no way to truly repay God for all that we have been given. But when God is the center of our world and possessions are in their proper place, we give of them as a way of thanking God for what we have.

Practice

Look carefully at everything you own and pretend that you are moving across the country and that every item you ship brings increased costs.

1. What items can you dispose of?

2. Are there clothes that no longer fit you?

3. Do you have boxes of things that have remained packed from a previous move?

4. Are you really going to read all of those books again?

5. Are there household items you no longer use?

6. Many of the items you have may be of use to someone else. Secondhand stores that use their income to help others, libraries in need of financial help, food banks, shelters, drop-in centers, and other places are often looking for a variety of items. Bring what you don't need to one of these places that really needs the resources.

7. In the future, before buying anything new, consider whether this is something you really need to own. Try to avoid buying things on impulse and give yourself a day or two to consider purchasing new items. See if the need to have a new item decreases over time.

What You Have Belongs to God

"For they [the brothers] believe not only that they themselves are not their own, but also that everything that they possess is consecrated to the Lord."

—The Twelve Books of John Cassian on the Institutes of the Coenobia

A friend of mine joined a monastery a couple of years ago and one of the things he had to do before entering the monastery was to pay off all his debts and give away almost everything he owned. It has been this way in religious communities since the earliest days of Christianity. One entered, and still enters, religious life with nothing to call one's own. What you have belongs to the community, which belongs to God.

Most of us would find this a difficult step to take in our lives and God does not ask us to give up every possession. Still, the reality is that everything we have is God's, a gift only on loan to us temporarily. As the old proverb says: "You can't take it with you." We are stewards, or caretakers, of those gifts while we are here, rather than the owners and controllers. As stewards we use some of what we have for the sake of God's work. If you are a church member you have probably heard of the concept of tithing—giving one-tenth of what you have or earn for religious purposes. The custom appears several times in the Old Testament. "Honor the Lord with your substance and with the first fruits of all your produce," says Proverbs 3:9. In other words, we give back to God the first and best fruits of what we have.

These tithes were considered to be not only one's duty, but holy to God. "All tithes from the land, whether the seed from the ground or the fruit from the tree, are the Lord's; they are holy to the Lord." (Leviticus 27:30) Tithes were used to help the poor, as in Deuteronomy 14:28–29. "Every third year you shall bring out the full tithe of your produce for that year, and store it within your towns; the Levites, because they have no allotment or inheritance with you, as well as the resident aliens, the orphans, and the widows in your towns, may come and eat their fill so that the Lord your God may bless you in all the work that you undertake."

Not all of us are ready—spiritually or financially—to offer 10 percent of what we have to God. But each of us can return something of our time, skills or talents, and resources—no matter how small. Over time, perhaps that gift will grow, but the act of giving itself is holy to God and God blesses any and all of our efforts to help those who are in need. If we view ourselves as God's stewards then sharing what we have becomes easy. If what we earn and what we possess is not ours in the first place then hoarding all of it for ourselves seems selfish and unacceptable. We have been given gifts that God intended us to share with others.

The word stewardship usually conjures up images of money for people, and though it can and does involve money many times, the concept is much larger. Stewardship involves giving of any resources you have. Those can just as easily be your time, energy, skills, and abilities as it is cash. Many of the remaining segments in this chapter focus on the way you can use your time and talent, so I'll focus here on what money we can give away. Most of us feel that we don't have much money to give and perhaps that is true. But one of the interesting ways to look at the money you can give to charities or religious purposes comes from the regular fund-raising efforts of my local radio station. A basic level membership, they remind listeners, costs about twelve cents a day. Even one of their highest regular level membership costs about thirty cents a day—less than a cup of coffee. I don't know about you, but I don't think twice about paying quite a bit for a good café au lait on a regular basis. If I gave up even a small fraction of those, I would have a tidy sum to give to those who need the basics of life far more than I need an extravagant cup of coffee. Stewardship of our money is about putting the needs of God's creation before that cup of coffee.

Practice

For many people giving away 10 percent of their salary seems impossible. If that seems the case to you, spend some time discerning what you feel you can give.

1. It may help you to think very specifically about the charities you want to support. Is there an organization or church that you feel would use your money in ways you think are vitally important?

2. Try to bring the issue of financial giving into your prayer time with God. What do you feel God is asking of you in terms of stewardship?

3. Look at what you spend during a given month. Are there small things you could give up that would make a big difference in your ability to give?

4. Set a percentage of your salary you know you can give each month and commit to this level of financial stewardship for a year's time. At the end of the year, reevaluate the decision and adjust as needed. Over time you may find that the percentage creeps up, and you are working closer and closer to tithing.

Give According to Your Abilities

"Be warm and merciful and let none go from you empty-handed. The least you can offer is your time and patience, your affection and your prayer."

—Rule for a New Brother

M any years ago, when I was working with the homeless of Berkeley, a wise woman taught me something I have never forgotten. On the streets of Berkeley and in other major cities in this country, one is constantly approached by people living on the streets who want money. It is easy to grow weary of these requests and to ignore those who make them; the problems of the homeless quickly become overwhelming. I found I simply could not give money to everyone who asked me for something. Wendy, who worked with the homeless for a living, understood the compassion fatigue that accompanies constant requests for assistance, but she taught me that there was something I could do, even when I could not or would not give money to an individual. More than being denied funds, she said, people on the street were deeply angered by being ignored. The least people could do, when approached, was to look at the person and say "no," rather than completely ignoring the person and the request and hurrying on by. In essence, she was teaching me what this rule says: "The least you can offer is your time and patience, your affection and your prayer."

Years later, another teacher in my life reinforced this message from a different perspective. Terry had preached a wonderful sermon about helping the oppressed. I could agree with all he said, but found my own gifts in this area to be lacking. While I had worked with the homeless a little in a variety of contexts, I found that the volunteer work drained me and made me irritable. I found little joy in giving, and I felt incredibly guilty that this was so. As I sat and talked to Terry about my guilt over not doing more for the poor he turned to me and said, "So you think God gave you the wrong gifts?" The question brought me up short, for Terry knew of my volunteer work with a religious computer network and the work I did managing bookstores. What he was telling me was to exercise the gifts as God gave them to me and not to wish for different ones. Each of us is called to serve in whatever way we can, rather than all of us being called to serve every single need that exists in our world.

Still, it is hard to confront all of the need in today's world. It takes little to overwhelm our ability to be compassionate these days. If you read a newspaper, watch the news, or even just look around you on the street daily, the basic human needs that go unmet can cause us to go numb to avoid pain. Often we feel, as if each of us, individually, must address or solve all of the problems we see, but that is simply not possible.

But it is still possible to grow in our capacity to serve others. Opportunities to help are all around us, but our ability to accept and act on them depends upon our relationship with God. When our own reservoirs are full, we are able to reach out in compassion to others. Few people who give greatly of themselves would actually count themselves as self-sacrificing, and they do not see themselves as martyrs either. They give and serve gladly, and perhaps if we cannot give of ourselves cheerfully, we are not yet ready to give at all. Service is our grateful response to a loving God, not a duty where we grit our teeth as we try to help.

Part of giving cheerfully is doing so with a clear sense of your own gifts. Each of us was created with different abilities. Paul writes of this in 1 Corinthians 12:4–6: "Now there are varieties of gifts, but the same Spirit; and there are varieties of services, but the same Lord; and there are varieties of activities, but it is the same God who activates all of them in everyone." God calls us to give of our own gifts, not of someone else's. By discerning what we are called to give and doing so to the best of our ability, we respond to the love of God for us and for others.

Practice

Spend some time discerning what kinds of gifts and service you have to offer by considering the following:

1. Recall times when you have assisted others and found the experience nurturing to yourself as well as to others. Is there any pattern to these experiences?

2. What experiences in caring for others or supporting causes has been a burden to you in the past? Which ones left you stripped of your own resources? Can you avoid these in the future?

3. Are there particular kinds of people you feel called to serve? Those who are homebound? In prison? Sick in the hospital or in nursing care? The homeless? The dying? What volunteer opportunities exist for working with these people?

4. Are there causes you feel called to help and support? The environment? Action for the poor and oppressed? For those with various serious illnesses? Children or women who have been abused? Animals in need of care or a home? What volunteer opportunities exist in these areas?

Once you have decided that you would like to be of more service to others and you have identified one or more opportunities to help, pray for God's guidance and support in the tasks you have chosen. If you find the opportunities you have chosen to accept sap your resources more than they nurture you on a regular basis, take the questions above to God in prayer again and try to listen for new direction.

Take Action Against Injustice

"You should not, however, remain speechless and mute in face of every wrong-doing or omission. At the right moment you should reprove, warn or exhort but always with patience and the desire to instruct."
—The Jerusalem Community Rule of Life

I have to admire a friend of mine who recently took on some volunteer work that seems very difficult and worthwhile to me. She is giving her time to an organization that helps abused and neglected children who have been removed from their parents. Acting as the child's advocate, she works with the child, the parents, and whoever else is involved, to help the judge appointed to the case determine what is in the best interests of the child. That is not always easy to figure out as there are always as many sides to the case as there are people involved. Her job is to be in contact with all the parties, help people understand what is needed, and work for change when possible, all the while shepherding the child through whatever parts of the legal system are necessary. To the best of her ability she has to remain neutral and try not to take sides, or at the minimum, avoid jumping to conclusions quickly. She has to try to be patient with all the parties involved, to reprove or warn when needed but always in the interest of instruction and the possibility of reconciling the family unit—or doing what is best in the long-term interests of the child. The work is never easy.

We are not all suited to this kind of volunteer work, but we are all called to stand in the face of oppression and hurtful acts. The call may come in the form of saying that we don't find it amusing when a joke makes fun of or stereotypes an ethnic group or sex, or in responding to a request for help from someone who is being hurt or abused. Perhaps we will need to stand up to our supervisor at work when conditions are poor or unethical decisions are being made. If we are paying attention there are numerous situations almost any day—in the news, at home, or at work—where our help could be invaluable.

We cannot, of course, respond to every injustice in the world every day. The Jerusalem Community Rule, a rule from a monastic community that deliberately lives in the city where it feels called to minister, suggests that we respond not to every single injustice, but that we stand up to at least some of them. Further, it asks us to pick the right moment to respond, and to "reprove, warn or exhort but always with patience and the desire to instruct." To do so requires so much more care than just being angry with injustice in the world. My friend, who works with the abused and neglected children, finds this to be difficult sometimes. She, and the other volunteers, find it hard not to be angry with parents, social workers, and others who have failed the children. Still, they know they will not get the results they desire by blasting various individuals with their anger. They might express that to each other, but they need to respond to the parents and other parties with patience and the desire to be helpful, to instruct. They need to pick the right time and place to reprove, warn, exhort or even teach; embarrassing a parent in public, for instance, is not likely to solve behavioral problems. Not every situation can be corrected, but the odds of achieving family reunification improve when the child's volunteer advocate can listen to all sides, but still stand against neglect or abuse out of love and not hatred.

The same is true in our workplaces, homes, and even in the political arena. If we see something amiss, if we see an injustice, we need to decide what is the right time and place and the best way to bring this to the attention of the perpetrator. Sometimes a private conversation works best; other times we will be forced to bring abuse and oppression into the public light of day. At other times, we will need to report the problem to those who are trained to help and perhaps live with the consequences of "tattling" on a loved one, colleague, or neighbor.

It can be hard to do this in a spirit of love and patience, and at times our own righteous anger will get the best of us. The prophets in the Old Testament were not exactly known for their moderate responses to people's disregard of God, and we will find ourselves sharing their feelings at times. Nonetheless, when we can recognize that those who abuse or oppress others are often suffering themselves, that they are in need of God's healing, as are the victims, we can begin to include them in our prayers and approach them in love instead of in hatred. In doing so we give up our own control and needs and let God be the agent of change, rather than trying to take all the burdens of injustice on our own shoulders.

Practice

Find a space of time in which to quiet yourself and review the events in your world for the last few days or longer. Are there injustices that you have witnessed but not addressed that come to mind? These could be issues in your workplace, home, or in the news right now. Do any of them seem to call to you specifically? If you find that you feel a great deal of energy or concern around any particular problem, perhaps this is one you are called to address. If you are willing to stand up to that injustice, think or journal about some of the following questions before deciding what you will do.

1. What is the nature of the injustice? Can you think of more than one way in which it might be viewed by the different participants?

2. Is there any research you need to do on the situation? Are there facts you are missing? Is there evidence to collect?

3. Can you hold all the different parties involved—the perpetrators as well as the victims—in prayer? Are you willing that God's will be done in the situation, even if that turns out to be different than your original goal?

4. What kinds of actions are appropriate in the situation? What can you see yourself doing?

5. Imagine the response you might receive if you follow
   through on your action plan. Can you live with that?

If you can answer the questions above and still feel called to
respond to a particular injustice put your plans into action
as appropriate.

CHAPTER TEN

Hospitality

"The source of hospitality is the heart of God who yearns to unite every creature within one embrace."
—The Rule of the Society of St. John the Evangelist

When she heard I was moving across the country an acquaintance of mine who lived in my state-to-be called me and offered to help me unpack and set up my new household. We knew each other only a little, mostly through a few brief business contacts over the years, and now we were going to be working for the same company. I gave her two months' notice of my arrival date and told her that she had plenty of time now to find some reason to get out of her overly kind offer. But she showed up as scheduled and spent two days helping me unload all the boxes, put everything away, and even hang the pictures. I was settled into my new home in record time, feeling a little less like a stranger than I had when I first arrived in my new city. I continue to be amazed and challenged by my friend's kindness; it was the essence of hospitality.

Hospitality is simply a matter of following the Golden

Rule: Do unto others as you would have them do unto you. Empathy is our primary tool. We place ourselves in someone else's situation and consider their needs. To meet their needs, to offer hospitality, involves sacrifice for us. Perhaps we let someone else have the last donut rather than eating it ourselves. Or we work extra hours to help out a colleague who is at home taking care of a sick child. Maybe we take time from our day to take the homeless person begging for food to the local diner for a meal. We will feel some of those sacrifices more deeply than we do others, but in meeting the needs of others, we find some of our own needs being met as well. Most of us have the image of hospitality being self-sacrificing and painful, and sometimes it is, but more often than not it satisfies our own needs and allows us to exercise the gifts God gave us. Offering hospitality can be one of the most deeply fulfilling activities we do.

Practicing hospitality, and even accepting it from others, often stretches us physically, emotionally, or spiritually. Welcoming the stranger, for instance, can be very difficult for some of us, challenging us to be open to new people and new situations. Being hospitable to those who are different from us, or even to the difficult periods in our own lives, requires a great deal from us. Giving other people space to live their lives sometimes requires that we curtail our own space or bad habits. All of these are opportunities to graciously consider what another might need, and all of them can stretch our own limits of compassion.

None of this need be done to the point of our own exhaustion; when we give too much all the time we are finally without the resources to give anymore. God does not call us to this kind of masochism, but rather to a careful discernment of our gifts for hospitality and then the exercise of those gifts in appropriate ways. There must be boundaries to our hospitality for our own sake and for the sake of those to whom we offer it; caring for another so completely that the person no longer does any self-care does not usually help either party.

Nonetheless, God calls us, on behalf of God, to help care for and offer kindness to all who surround us locally and globally. We are God's hands in this work, and we have been given all the gifts we need to accomplish it. No matter who we are, there are gifts of hospitality at our disposal waiting to be used.

Practice Hospitality to All

"It is Christ himself whom we receive in a guest. Let us learn to welcome; . . . let hospitality be liberal and exercised with discernment."

—The Rule of Taizé

I am not always the bravest soul about going places I have never been before. I know that my life will be dull if I do not go new places every so often, but when it actually comes time to do it I often find excuses to avoid the trip. Fundamentally I am somewhat shy, and I find it hard to meet new people, so I avoid doing it when I can. Still, one night last year I decided to conquer my anxieties.

I had seen an advertisement in the local paper for a Taizé prayer service, which involves the chanting and meditation that I find soul-sustaining. So I swallowed hard and ventured to a church where I knew no one. Much to my surprise a gracious woman about my own age spotted me immediately and took it upon herself to introduce herself and to inquire about me. After a brief conversation she invited me to sit with her during the service and made a point of introducing me to others after the service was over. She did all of this in so unobtrusive a way, with so much genuine welcome, that my anxiety about being in a sanctuary full of strangers dissipated entirely and I felt completely at home. I came home that evening not only thankful for the welcome of this wonderful woman, but with gratitude for God for putting me in her path. The woman has since become a friend and the congregation has become a home, first and foremost because of their immense hospitality to me and to other "strangers." They treat people they don't know as other children of God, welcoming them to share their worship and life together, and in doing so they are enriched themselves.

Such a warm welcome can be a surprise to many of us. Many parts of our lives and many of our institutions are structured to help us separate "us" from "them." In grammar school we knew that some kids would be chosen first for team sports while others would always be selected last. In high school we knew the difference between the "in" crowd and the less popular students. We knew which kids were really smart and which ones were not, and we carried that into college with us. And in business, the management separates itself often from nonmanagement, keeping track of "us" and "them." In all of these situations hospitality is generally ignored. If we are the best and the brightest we are taught to disassociate from those who are not so quick. If we are management, we often fail to take much notice of the needs of those who are staff. Hospitality toward others is not expected, and sometimes not even encouraged.

Those who live in big and busy cities have also become accustomed to living with little expectation of hospitality. In fact, in some urban areas the grouchy behavior has become a sort of status symbol. Several television shows in the last few years have featured lead or occasional characters who are almost lovable in their disdain for others, as if rude and insulting behavior were really pleasant to experience. We have to be reminded by bumper stickers to "practice random acts of kindness" and hospitality comes as a surprise to us when we encounter it. But if we live our lives focused on God, rather than ourselves, we are asked to practice hospitality. The Gospel of Matthew tells us this most forcefully. Those who have practiced hospitality, Jesus invites to inherit the kingdom, using these words:

"'... For I was hungry and you gave me food, I was thirsty and you gave me something to drink, I was a stranger and you welcomed me, I was naked and you gave me clothing, I was sick and you took care of me, I was in prison and you visited me.'

"Then the righteous will answer him, 'Lord, when was it that we saw you hungry and gave you food, or thirsty and gave you something to drink? And when was it that we saw you a stranger and welcomed you, or naked and gave you clothing? And when was it we saw you sick or in prison and visited you?'

"And the king will answer them, 'Truly I tell you, just as you did it to one of the least of these who are members of my family, you did it to me.'" (Matthew 25:35–40)

Those who failed to offer these types of kindness, Jesus condemns. There is little question that we are being asked in the most forceful way possible to practice hospitality to the rest of humankind, the other members of God's family. We are to welcome the stranger, to put our own interest aside and offer what care, assistance, or comfort is needed. No matter how meager we think our resources are, we are to offer what we can.

Practice

Find an opportunity to offer hospitality to someone else on a daily basis: The acts can be large or small; it makes no difference as long as you find some way to show at least one person some hospitality each day. Some suggestions might include:

- Treating a client or customer like an honored guest
- Treating a family member to a special day or evening
- Volunteering to feed the homeless and hungry in the local soup kitchen and remembering that those you serve are your guests
- Looking for a child who needs mentoring
- Looking for the person in a social situation who is lonely or uncomfortable and finding ways to make him or her feel more at home
- Treating an interruption in your schedule as an opportunity instead of a nuisance
- Complimenting someone on an accomplishment
- Comforting someone who is sad.

Accept Others As They Are

"Don't be irritated by the brother who sings off-key."
—Rule for a New Brother

One of my favorite events during Advent is the Lessons and Carols church service. Stories from the Bible are read while carols are sung by the choir and the congregation; the service is simple and often quite beautiful. Several years ago I was at this service at Grace Cathedral in San Francisco, a place I go when I want to be surrounded by beauty and wonderful sound. But as the congregation rose to sing its first hymn an awful voice right behind me shattered the beauty. This man was not only singing off-key, he sang off-key with gusto, enthusiasm, and loud volume, and I found it incredibly distracting. Repeatedly I reminded myself to adopt a more charitable attitude toward this poor singer. I lectured myself on the need to sink into my own prayers and stop being so irritated by his voice, but I found it very difficult. As the communion part of the service neared, we were all invited to take communion. A station for healing prayers was also set up for anyone who wished them. This man with the terrible voice went up and took communion, then promptly moved over to the railing for healing prayers. He knelt down and accepted the ministrations of the priest and returned to his seat with an absolutely beatific smile on his face. It was clear that he had come to this service out of love for God and out of some deep need that had been met. He returned to his seat and continued to sing poorly and loudly for the remainder of the service, but somehow my heart had melted a little bit and I no longer minded as much. He had become a child of God in my eyes, instead of just a man with a bad singing voice.

Our spiritual lives are full of challenges by "brothers who sing off-key." In all likelihood most of us encounter people daily who do things in a way that we find less than perfect, people whose habits irritate us. It is easy to bristle, either aloud or silently, and wish that others did things as well as we do, or that at the very least they would do them elsewhere, out of our sight.

I saw a bumper sticker once that read: "God loves you and I'm trying." I would bet that the bumper sticker was meant to be sarcastic, but there is a wonderful grain of truth in it. What would happen if we were to look carefully at the person who annoys us and pray: "God loves you and I'm trying" or even just "God loves you"? The acceptance of others begins by recognizing that each of us is a beloved child of God. If we can see that in each other we may be able to better appreciate the differences between us. We may even grow to love the differences. At the very least, if we can see what is precious within each other, we can begin to offer compassion instead of criticism.

Acceptance, however, does not mean that we become a Pollyanna and see the world only in the rosiest way. Nor are we called to accept abuse and injustice. A wife being beaten by her husband is not called to practice acceptance of her husband's behavior. None of us is called to stand by and let others be abused, starved, or harmed. Practicing acceptance means that we try to see past the behaviors of others and look for what is good and wonderful within them. But it does not mean that we allow them to continue to hurt us or others.

Acceptance can be a difficult practice to develop, since it is hard to control the way we feel about events and people. To deny the way we actually feel does little good and is not actually acceptance. What we must do is to be willing to see differently and then practice that. We must see the man with the poor voice through God's eyes, rather than our own, and then acceptance comes much more easily.[41]

It is not easy to practice acceptance in today's culture. We are accustomed to enjoying wisecracks and jokes at the expense of others on television, in ads and movies, and most of us hear plenty of gossip during any given day. It is easier to laugh at others or simply stew in anger at them than it is to change our own perception of their difficulties. In the end, however, it takes more energy to be annoyed than it does to change our own response to a difficult situation. If we must stop and get irritated every time a brother or sister sings off-key, we will have little time to enjoy the wonder of what actually surrounds us.

Practice

Try an experiment sometime when you are dealing with an event or a person that frustrates or annoys you. In the beginning you may need some distance from what angers you in order to try this, though it will get easier and more automatic with practice.

1. First, look carefully at the situation and see if change is possible. If it is, go ahead and do what you can to effect the changes.

2. If that is genuinely not possible, notice first whether or not you are willing to see things differently. You may find that you are too upset or annoyed to try this right now, and if so, wait until you are ready to try on a new perspective.

3. Sit quietly and let the image of the person or situation that distresses you come into your mind. As you look at it in your imagination, try to look past what disturbs you and find other characteristics that feel better to you. This may take some time to do, particularly if the situation has been troublesome for a while, but spend some time really looking for the brighter side of this person and see if you can't find even one small thing that is positive.

4. If you find this particularly difficult, you might ask others to help you. Perhaps friends who know the situation react differently to it, and can tell you what they like about the person or event.

5. Pray for the one who irritates you.

6. Once you have something positive in mind, try to remember that when you encounter the difficulty again. See if you can see this person as God sees him or her. If you can, let that image change your own response to what is happening.

7. Over time you may be able to add other positive characteristics to your list. It is even possible that

you will actually come to enjoy someone who has annoyed you in the past. But the goal is to learn to see others through God's eyes, to accept them just as they are.

Expect Abundance

"If we give freely of ourselves, we should expect abundant gifts in return, according to Christ's promise. We should enter into our ministries expecting to receive as much or more than we give."
—The Rule of the Society of St. John the Evangelist

Maybe this rule surprises you. After all, most of us were taught as children that it was more blessed to give than to receive. It was especially blessed (we were told) to give selflessly, with no expectation of gaining anything in return. We admire people, such as Mother Teresa, who seem to give so much and ask for so little in return. So why are we being advised here to enter into our ministries and our lives expecting to gain as much as we give?

The truth, however, is that none of us is able to give with complete selflessness. Mother Teresa found Christ in all of the people she helped, which deepened her own relationship to God. Showing hospitality to others also makes us feel good; we have an opportunity to use our gifts or we find ourselves growing and stretching in some way. Put very simply, practicing hospitality often feels good to the person who shows the kindness. Some years ago on the popular television sitcom *Friends*, Joey challenged Phoebe to do even one act that was completely selfish—something that didn't leave her feeling pleased with herself. Phoebe always did generous acts, so he wanted to see if she had a selfish bone in her. Try as she might Phoebe could not manage to do something that no one knew about or that didn't leave her feeling good because she had done something to help someone else.

We can, therefore, use our gifts and offer our hospitality in the expectation that we will receive as much as or more that we give. But we do not do that as the bellboy in a comedy might. To offer hospitality while putting our hand out for the tip is not to offer hospitality at all. We assist others and offer our gifts to the world in the expectation that the act itself will be rewarding in some way, but without knowing what the reward will be. We do not have our hand out in expectation of being given a dollar for carrying a suitcase, nor do we sneer when we are given fifty cents instead of the dollar we expected. When we give of ourselves, more often than not, we receive something in return. That does not mean that we expect to receive extravagant gifts, become wealthy, or even be rewarded in some way that tells the whole world how wonderful we are. The gifts we receive are usually more subtle. We feel some satisfaction in helping someone else. Or we enjoy finding that we have gifts, skills, or abilities that we didn't know were in us. Perhaps our extension of hospitality allows us to grow spiritually and deepens our own relationship with God. Even failures can sometimes be a gift, a pathway to eventual gain in our lives.

We also need to be cautious of offering ourselves in situations where our help or gifts are not wanted, or when doing so places us in physical danger that serves no greater purpose. Forcing our gifts and ministry on others or martyring ourselves for no reason other than self-glorification are not ways of practicing hospitality. In situations such as these we often find the practice of hospitality wears us down; if it continues long enough, we may need to leave that particular situation or stop offering help where it is not wanted.

Outside of these situations, however, we should expect abundance. Parker Palmer in his book *The Active Life* does a very helpful analysis of the story in the Gospel of Mark about the fishes and the loaves. Five thousand people have gathered to hear Jesus speak, and as evening falls Jesus asks the disciples to feed the crowd. The disciples immediately assume scarcity and cannot imagine how they can feed so many people. Jesus, on the other hand, assumes abundance, collects what food there is in the crowd and miraculously feeds everyone. We are challenged to be like Jesus in this story, to assume that there will be enough of whatever is needed, to believe in abundance over scarcity.

Practice

Part of the ability of expecting abundance in return for the gift of our hospitality is to begin noticing how often we already receive as much or more than we have given. It is so much simpler to focus on the things that annoyed us or the things we did not receive during the course of a day than it is to notice the gifts that came our way.

1. Take some time at the end of each day to look at the moments during which you offered your gifts or hospitality to others and the responses you received.

2. Were you thanked for your assistance? Did you experience a sense of satisfaction or peacefulness for having been available to someone else?

3. Did your hospitality relieve the burden of someone else or make a system work better? Did the act of hospitality help you stretch or grow? Did it deepen your own sense of doing acts God calls you to do?

All of these, and more, are the gifts we receive as a result of our ministry. By noticing them daily, you will grow in the ability to expect abundance in your daily life.

Be Awake to the Dangers of Unlimited Hospitality

"Be wide awake to the dangers of unlimited hospitality . . . You might reach saturation point and end by becoming superficial, distracted or monopolized. Do not be nowhere in your effort to be everywhere, or attentive to no one simply because you are running after everyone."

—The Jerusalem Community Rule of Life

For some of us, the problem is not practicing hospitality, but learning to offer it more wisely. Sometimes we bring our own needs for control or accomplishment to the act of hospitality—the number of people we serve per day or the efficiency with which we meet their needs becomes more important than actual human contact with others. Others practice hospitality as if they were meeting some obligation: God calls them to help others, so they do. They meet the letter of the law without addressing the spirit of it at all. This can lead to approaching those who need our services, help, or our presence as factory workers would approach widgets on an assembly line. Instead of taking the time to listen to the real needs of another and respond appropriately, we listen for a moment, make a quick decision, act upon it, and move on. This is rarely actual hospitality, but simply the completion of something on our to-do list. It does not normally meet the needs of the person before us, and it does not feed us either.

Almost all the monastic rules recommend the practice of hospitality, but they also all warn of the dangers of practicing hospitality without careful discernment. The rules of most monasteries advise the residents to greet guests as they would greet Christ. To do that monks and nuns must be quiet within and able to discover the needs of each guest. Rather than having a checklist of things to tell every single guest and doing that as quickly as possible with everyone, the monk or nun needs to listen for the individual needs of those who come to visit. He or she tries to be a nonanxious presence for the visitor, to determine the needs and provide whatever resources possible. Providing more than is required is often not any more helpful than running through a checklist of things to tell visitors and abandoning them for the remainder of their stay. In both cases the needs of the stranger, though perhaps met superficially, are not addressed at a deep level. Neither the guest nor the monk or nun have met God in the other person.

There is a wonderful example of this lack of discernment in the Danish movie based on Isak Dinesen's novel *Babette's Feast*. Two elderly Lutheran sisters, Martine and Philippa, spend their days feeding others in their village who, for whatever reason, need assistance with food. They cook and bring their soup around to the different residents, but they do so without much actual hospitality. Their stop to provide food is brief; they enter, provide the food, and without any conversation leave the needy person to eat alone. Then Martine and Philippa move on to the next house. They fulfill the law by doing as they believe God calls them, but they do so with little love or hospitality.

One stormy night a French woman, Babette, comes to the door. She has been sent to the sisters to live with them and be their housekeeper. She does this for fourteen years, at which point she wins a great deal of money in the lottery. Rather than leaving the sisters and setting up a life of her own, she throws a huge feast for the sisters and their friends. Babette, it is revealed, is a gourmet cook and she spends all of her 10,000 francs on a French dinner fit for kings. The dour sisters and their friends are determined not to enjoy the meal as pleasures of the body are inappropriate and perhaps even threatening to the soul. As they eat, however, they all find it impossible not to experience the grace of the elegant meal before them, and they begin to patch up old wounds between them and to experience genuine love for one another. Babette's dinner, given without any expectation of reciprocity, is the gift of grace and hospitality in the lives of these village people and the sisters—it enables the community to heal itself and experience real love.

Babette's gift was the result of careful discernment on her part. She gave what she was uniquely qualified to give—a feast that used her cooking skills—and she gave that gift to those she thought would benefit from it. We are asked to do likewise with our hospitality. Rather than trying to be all things to all people at all times, or trying to be busy about hospitality every moment in order to meet the letter of the law, we are called to discover what our own gifts are and to use them to benefit others who need those gifts. This usually entails acknowledging that we cannot be helpful in all situations.

Practice

Spend some time discovering what gifts you might have for hospitality.

1. What kind of people are you most attracted to? What gifts might you offer them? Those gifts might be organizational or management ones, artistic ones, various abilities such as cooking, building or others. Try to think back to times when you enjoyed helping someone and see if you can find common threads in the various situations.

2. Try, also, to think of times when offering hospitality drained you rather than fed you. What common characteristics can you find in these situations?

3. As you contemplate opportunities to offer hospitality in your daily life, try to discern where you can offer it well.

Give Others Space

"No one shall enter the cell of his neighbor without first knocking."

—The Rule of Pachomius

Within each culture there is a sense of personal space that is required between people if everyone is to be comfortable. Perhaps you have been in the same situation I have on occasion, and found yourself talking with someone from another country who has a different sense of this than you do and who stands much too close to you in conversation. You keep backing up a step or two until your back is up against the wall. It is nearly impossible to focus on the conversation because you are so uncomfortable.

We have an almost innate sense of the space each of us requires in this life. When talking to anyone with whom we are not intimately involved we need several feet around us in order to be comfortable. This goes beyond our physical senses, however. We also need emotional and spiritual space from others. We need that room to think our own thoughts, to sort things out, and sometimes even to relax. We have probably all experienced the discomfort of having someone who is overly familiar with us too early in the relationship or the salesperson who is so persistent that we want to scream. Fending off this kind of intrusion into our space is no less difficult than dealing with the person who stands too close to us.

It is not hard for any of us to know when someone has violated our physical, emotional, or spiritual space. It may be more difficult to recognize how often we do this to others. I find that I am most oblivious to the space of others when I am particularly excited or angry. Sometimes when I have something that really thrills me I just want to tell others about it, even if they are busy at that moment. The same is true occasionally when I am very upset about something. My anger can feel like a creature inside of me who just wants to get out desperately, and I can end up ignoring the needs of others as I spew my frustration. I can forget "to knock before entering" sometimes.

There are many other ways we invade the space of others in everyday life. Interrupting others is a way of not "knocking before entering." We are so involved with our own reply to someone else that we don't even listen to the rest of what they have to say before we begin to tell them what we think. Giving advice, particularly unwanted advice, is another way of not giving others their space. When we decide that we know what is best for someone else and try to force our opinion on them we are not practicing hospitality.

Overfamiliarity with others too soon in a relationship can be another way of not "knocking first." Being hugged deeply by a total stranger is usually very uncomfortable and invasive. Likewise, calling someone by a nickname that they have not used themselves, or failing to use someone's title when it is important to them, can be very annoying to the person being addressed. People who have just met me, for instance, sometimes call me "Deb" instead of Debra. More often than not, that feels as if someone has assumed a familiarity that is inappropriate at the beginning of our relationship. Yet it is not uncommon for us to shorten other people's names or change them into a more familiar form.

We can also invade people's space spiritually if we are not careful. We ask people to confide in us too readily at times, to reveal more of themselves than is comfortable. In group settings such as retreats or spirituality workshops this sometimes happens when people are broken up into small groups; for people who do not wish to share, the pressure of being in a small group can be excruciating. Other times people are asked to engage in rituals or activities without being asked for their permission first. Asking someone to try even the simplest of new prayer practices without asking their permission first is a form of "entering without knocking." This is particularly true in group situations, but can happen with individuals as well.

Sometimes these methods of invading others are done unconsciously; we do not mean to be offensive. More often than not they come from the fact that we are focused on ourselves, instead of on the person before us, or because we assume we know what is best for someone else. When our lives are centered on God, however, it is harder for us to be oblivious to the needs of others or to assume that we can make decisions for them. With our focus on God, we are able to be hospitable but also humble. We know ourselves as one of God's beloved, no more and no less important than any other. Part of hospitality is treating everyone else with respect; we do not enter their space without knocking and obtaining permission first.

Practice

So often we invade other people's physical, emotional, or spiritual space without intending to; we are unaware that we have done so. Some of the ways we do this are completely spontaneous and happen only once, while other times they are habitual (e.g., interrupting others while speaking).

1. Begin by trying to become aware of ways in which you "enter without knocking." Some of the ways you might do this are listed above, but watch for others.

2. If you sense someone drawing back from you, becoming silent in your presence, try to see if you have done something that might feel invasive to the other person.

3. Make a list of ways in which you have invaded the space of others for future reference.

4. Although it sounds like a childhood game, try something very simple to help you curb these behaviors, particularly ones that you do repeatedly. For each invasive act you perform, whether intentional or without thinking, put a quarter or a dollar into a bank. The act of atoning with your money for these acts will help you to become more conscious of the acts you do, and will help you see quite graphically how you are doing.

5. After a few weeks of this you will probably find yourself interrupting others less often, giving less advice, or whatever it is that you do habitually. When you find that you are not putting much money in the

bank anymore, give the money you have collected away to a charity. Continue to practice "knocking before entering," and revert to putting money in the bank again if you find yourself slipping backward in the future.

Accept What Exists

"[The new convert] ought to be imbued with humility above all things so that he may not do his own will . . . but be prepared for all things; whatever happens he must be mindful to be patient in tribulation."
—The Rule of the Four Fathers

Perhaps one of the hardest parts of practicing hospitality is to be as welcoming as possible of difficult times in our lives. This does not mean that we seek out or revel in hard periods of time; masochism is not what God asks of us. It does mean that we try to befriend the bad days, weeks, or years and try to learn from them what we can. It may also mean that we use these times to grow closer to God, accepting God's hospitality and concern for us, no matter what the circumstances.

Some years ago, for instance, I was confronted with the possibility that I might have a brain tumor. After some weeks of testing and anxiety I learned that I did not have a tumor, but I went through a considerable number of sleepless nights before learning that. The whole experience is one that I would not wish on anyone, but it is also an experience that has shaped my life in wonderful ways and I am grateful. I went from being in deep shock on first hearing the news, to a great deal of darkness and fear, and finally to a place of deep quiet in which I felt God's presence as I never had before. By the time of the final testing, before I knew what the results would be, I was confident that whatever the outcome, God was with me and would provide me with whatever strength was needed. The anxiety I felt, while not completely gone, was largely replaced by a sense of quiet waiting and a certainty that—one way or another—all would be well.

One of the things that sometimes prevents us from experiencing God in the bleak times of our lives is the underlying fear, encouraged by some schools of theological thought, that God might be inflicting these periods on us as punishment for something we have done. I do not subscribe to that school of thinking, nor do I find it to be biblically based. God, in the book of Job, expressly denies that Job is being punished for anything, and states that we human beings cannot begin to know the ways of God. Therefore, suffering simply exists, and is not the will of God for our lives. Still, we can find ourselves growing emotionally and spiritually during the hard periods of our lives.

Maybe you've heard some version of the phrase "Life is hard. And then you die." There are days when the world feels like this for all of us, but the saying misses an important middle step. Life *is* hard, but the difficulties are frequently what challenge us to see our lives from a new perspective. Hard days can be the ones that enable us to grow in faith, compassion, strength, and understanding. I am not suggesting that you accept abusive treatment from others as spiritual discipline, but in many harsh situations we can choose to complain and be miserable or we can choose to find grace within the hardship. Being diagnosed with a terminal illness, for instance, can be the motivation for someone to mend torn relationships and to come to understand his or her utter reliance on God. Living through a difficult relationship or job can teach us strength and help us focus on finding better living situations. Particularly when we find ourselves living in hardships that are, at least to some level, self-imposed (a bad marriage, job, and so on), we have the opportunity to look at ourselves and explore what keeps us in these less-than-ideal circumstances; this can be the motivation we need to make changes in how we perceive ourselves and others. Experiencing trials can also make us more compassionate. At the same time, it may make our offers of comfort more readily acceptable to others who recognize that we have also suffered and know the experience.

Suffering is always an unwelcome guest in our lives, but none of us will escape periods of sadness, pain, and depression for the whole of our existence. And we have a right to dislike them, to complain and be frustrated that they don't pass soon enough or at all. But we are also challenged to accept these times as much as possible, for they are also moments when God may feel closest to us, moments when we can grow enormously. As Caroline Westerhoff writes in her book on the boundaries of hospitality: "Every time I am willing to stand calmly in the face of mystery, knowing that I finally can neither control nor manage it, I know I have realized a small measure of spiritual growth."[42] We do not need to pretend to enjoy these times, but the more we can open ourselves to the possibilities for change and renewal, the richer will be our existence.

Practice

1. The next time you have a difficult day or period of time, take time to pray to God and make all your complaints known. After you have finished expressing your anger or frustration, however, take some time to ask yourself what you might be able to learn from your suffering. Is it challenging you to do something differently? Does it push you to deepen your faith, develop more patience, let go of your need to control things?

2. Look at the difficult situation as an opportunity for growth in your life and try to determine how you might grow and embrace the possibilities in front of you.

Accept Hospitality from Others

"And each one should confidently make known his need to the other, so that he might find what he needs and minister it to him."

—The Earlier Rule of St. Francis

The majority of this chapter has focused on what it means to be hospitable to others, but some of us actually find it harder to accept hospitality than to give it. Learning to graciously receive hospitality is as much a spiritual discipline, however, as providing others with this gift. When we cannot accept the help others give us, when we growl in response to even being offered help, we end up being rude to others and making our own life harder. We reject the gifts that others would share with us, but more important, we turn away one of the gifts God offers us; we are being ungrateful.

I remember one night many years ago when an allergic reaction gave me trouble with my breathing. I was not gasping for air, but I was not comfortable during the night either, and was reasonably anxious about my condition since I didn't know what had brought it on. Not being able to breathe easily left me feeling a bit panicked. In the morning I called my doctor and made an appointment to see him right away. I felt too weak and dizzy to drive so I called a friend to take me to the appointment. Meanwhile, my next door neighbor and dear friend came over and found that I had had a difficult night. As a nurse, she was helpful and caring until it was time for me to go to the doctor's office, but when I came home I found her at my door in tears. "Don't you ever spend a night like that again and not call me," she said, in great distress. It hadn't even occurred to me to call her in the middle of the night—that seemed like such a rude thing to do unless it was an emergency. But she saw it differently and was terribly hurt that I had not asked for help.

Often we fail to accept hospitality and assistance from others because it seems like some sort of weakness on our part to do so. Many of us live with the idea that we must be superhuman and able to navigate every aspect of our life without any assistance from others. To need help is to be exposed as weak and ineffectual, unable to cope. Others equate accepting help with giving up control, with letting things unfold differently than they might have planned. Unfortunately, to need assistance sometimes is to be human, a fate none of us can escape. To believe and act as if we can do everything for ourselves is to equate ourselves with being God.

Others of us have trouble accepting hospitality and help because we feel we are undeserving. Perhaps someone is offering us a gift we cannot return. Maybe we're just so used to taking care of others that we can't switch gears when we need help ourselves. Others were raised or had some experience in their life that left them feeling undeserving of kindness and hospitality under any circumstances. The truth is that at some level none of us earns or deserves the gifts that come our way, and paradoxically we do. Take, for instance, the parable of the Prodigal Son (Luke 15:11ff). Rather arrogantly he asks for his inheritance from his still-living father and then squanders it through fast living. Without food or a way to live he returns home ready to beg forgiveness and ask to be accepted as a servant in his father's household. He doesn't get the chance to beg, however, since his father rushes to meet him and welcomes him homes effusively. The prodigal son's older brother is furious, since the younger brother has lived foolishly and does not seem to have to pay the consequences, while the older brother has lived righteously all his life. The boy's father, however, insists on celebrating the return of the lost son, deserved or not. Like the prodigal son we are welcomed home and given gifts, deserved or not, and our own sense of thankfulness to God demands that we accept them graciously. Perhaps we cannot return the kindness of a particular person, but nothing prevents us from doing a kindness to someone else out of gratitude for what has been done for us by others.

Practice

Long ago a friend of mine commented that many of us fail to deal well with hospitality, compliments, and assistance. According to my friend, most of us have a vulture on our shoulder that scoops up compliments and offers of assistance that come our way. Rather than responding with *thank you* we reject the compliment or turn away the hospitality. Instead of letting someone carry one of the three bags of groceries that fill our arms, we say something like, "Oh, it's okay. I've got them," and struggle along. The vulture enjoys the good and kind words and offers and we pretend they never came our way at all.

1. Think back to some of the compliments or offers of assistance that have come your way recently. What was your first response to them?

2. If you wanted to say something other than *thank you* to them, and particularly if you rebuffed the kindness in any way, try to explore why that was so. What would happen if you accepted gracious words and deeds?

3. In the future, practice saying thank you and accepting the gifts God sends you.

RULES CITED AND SOURCES

The Rule of St. Augustine
Tarsicus J. Van Bravel, OSA (commentary and introduction). Translated by Raymond Canning, OSA. *The Rule of Saint Augustine*. Kalamazoo, Michigan: Cistercian Publications, 1984.

Basil (c. 330–379)
Translated by Sr. M. Monica Wegner. *Writings: Volume 1: Ascetical Works*. New York: Fathers of the Church Inc., 1950.

Rule of St. Benedict (c. 480–547)
Fry, Timothy, O.S.B., editor. *The Rule of St. Benedict in English*. Collegeville, Minnesota: The Liturgical Press, 1982.

John Cassian (c. 365–435)
Cassian, John. *The Twelve Proofs of John Cassian on the Institutes of the Coenobia, and the Remedies for the Eight Principal Faults*. From the Web site: ccel.wheaton.edu/fathers/NPNF2-11/jcassian/inpref-6.txt

Rule of the Céli Dé
The Rule of Cormac Mac Ciolionáin
The Rule of Colmcille
Maidín, Uniseann, OCR. *The Celtic Monk: Rules and Writings of Early Irish Monks*. Kalamazoo, Michigan: Cistercian Publications, 1996.

The Rule of the Four Fathers
Franklin, Carmela Vircillo, and Havener, Ivan, O.S.B., and
Francis, J. Alcuin, O.S.B. *Early Monastic Rules: The Rules of
the Fathers and the Regula Orientalis*. Collegeville, Minnesota:
The Liturgical Press, 1982.

The Earlier Rule of St. Francis
The Rule of St. Clare
Translation and introduction by Regis J. Armstrong. O.F.M.
Cap., and Ignatius C. Bradley, O.F.M. *Francis and Clare: The
Complete Works*. New York: Paulist Press, 1982.

Hermits of Bethlehem
*Hermits of Bethlehem. A Way of Desert Spirituality: The Plan
of Life of the Hermits of Bethlehem*. Staten Island, New York:
Alba House, 1998.

The Jerusalem Community Rule of Life
Anonymous. *The Jerusalem Community Rule of Life*. Mahwah,
New Jersey: Paulist Press, 1985.

The Rule of the Master
Eberle, Luke, translator. *The Rule of the Master*. Kalamazoo,
Michigan: Cistercian Publications, 1977.

Rule for a New Brother
van der Looy, H. *Rule for a New Brother*. Springfield, Illinois:
Templegate Publishers, 1976.

The Rules of Pachomius
Veilleux, Armand (translation and introduction). *Pachomian
Koinonia: Volume 2: Pachomian Chronicles and Rules*. Kala-
mazoo, Michigan: Cistercian Publications, Inc., 1981.

The Rule of the Secular Franciscan Order
Catechism by Fr. Conelio Mota Ramos, O.F.M., and translated
by Fr. Felipe Baldonado, O.F.M. Instructions compiled by Cap-
uchin Friars and Secular Franciscans of the Province of St. Mary
and edited by Fr. Zachary Grant, O.F.M. Cap. *The Rule of the
Secular Franciscan Order: With a Catechism and Instructions.*
Quincy, Illinois: Franciscan Press, 1980.

The Rule of the Society of St. John the Evangelist
Anonymous. *The Rule of the Society of St. John the Evangelist.*
Boston, Massachusetts: Cowley Publications, 1997.

The Rule of Taizé
Brother Roger. *The Rule of Taizé*. New York: The Seabury
Press, 1968.

NOTES

[1]This historical overview is necessarily shortened and simplified. For a more detailed description of the development of early monasticism, see C. H. Lawrence, *Medieval Monasticism: Forms of Religious Life in Western Europe in the Middle Ages* (London and New York: Longman, 1984). The first three chapters of this book provide a vivid and detailed account of the beginnings of the monastic movement and the development of rules.

[2]This is not a particularly new practice in the world. Buddhists and Jews preceded Christians in going away from the world to meet God more deeply.

[3]For a collection of early Irish rules see Uniseann Ó Maidin, OCR, *The Celtic Monk: Rules and Writings of Early Irish Monks* (Kalamazoo, Michigan: Cistercian Publications, 1996).

[4]C. H. Lawrence, p. 45.

[5]See *The Rule of the Society of St. John the Evangelist* (Boston, Massachusetts: Cowley Publications, 1997).

[6]Margaret Guenther, *Toward Holy Ground: Spiritual Directions for the Second Half of Life* (Boston, Massachusetts: Cowley Publications, 1995), p. 64.

[7]I am indebted to Dr. Joseph Driskill for this exercise, both as it was taught to me in his class and as it appears in his book *Protestant Spiritual Exercises: Theology, History, and Practice* (Harrisburg, Pennsylvania: Morehouse Publishing, 1999), pp. 88–91.

[8]Regis J. Armstrong, O.F.M. CAP, and Ignatius C. Brady, O. F. M., translators, *Francis and Clare: the Complete Works* (Mahwah, New Jersey: Paulist Press, 1982), pp. 133–34.

[9]Anonymous, *The Rule of the Master*, translated by Luke Eberle (Kalamazoo, Michigan: Cistercian Publications, Inc., 1977), p. 173.

[10]C. H. Lawrence, *Medieval Monasticism: Forms of Religious Life in Western Europe in the Middle Ages* (London and New York: Longman, 1984) p. 10.

[11]Bill Williams, *Manna in the Wilderness: A Harvest of Hope* (Harrisburg, Pennsylvania: Morehouse Publishing, 1999), p. 52.

[12]Anonymous, *The Rule of the Society of St. John of the Evangelist* (Boston: Cowley Publications, 1997), p. 44.

[13]Brother Lawrence, translated by John J. Delaney, *The Practice of the Presence of God* (New York: Doubleday, 1977), p. 40.

[14]H. van der Looy, *Rule for a New Brother* (Springfield, Illinois: Templegate Publishers, 1976), p. 72.

[15]Anonymous, *The Rule of the Society of St. John the Evangelist* (Boston: Cowley Publications, 1997), p. 45.

[16]Capuchin Friars and Secular Franciscans of the Province of St. Mary, edited by Fr. Zachary Grant, O.F.M. Cap., *The Rule of the Secular Franciscan Order: With a Catechism and Instructions* (Quincey, Illinois: Franciscan Press, 1980), p. 29.

[17]Norvene Vest, *Friend of the Soul: A Benedictine Spirituality of Work* (Boston: Cowley Publications, 1997), p. 42.

[18]*The Book of Common Prayer* (New York: The Church Hymnal Corporation, 1979), p. 261.

[19]Anonymous, *The Jerusalem Community Rule of Life* (Mahwah, New Jersey: Paulist Press, 1985), pp. 19–20.

[20]John Cassian, *The Twelve Proofs of John Cassian on the Institutes of the Coenobia* (Web site: www.ccel.wheaton.edu/fathers/NPNF2-11/jcassian/inpref-6:txt), Book 4, Chapter 20.

[21]Lent is the forty days, plus Sundays, that precedes Easter.

[22]See description of the lectionary on page 138.

[23]Two excellent books that provide much more detail about the process of *lectio divina* are: Macrina Wiederkehr, *The Song of the Seed: A Monastic Way of Tending the Soul* (New York: HarperCollins, 1995); and Norvene Vest, *Gathered in the Word: Praying the Scripture in Small Groups* (Nashville: Upper Room Books, 1996).

[24]Eugene L. Romano, *A Way of Desert Spirituality: The Plan of Life of the Hermits of Bethlehem* (Staten Island, New York: Alba House, 1998), pp. 4–5.

[25]Robert Wuthnow, *After Heaven: Spirituality in America Since the 1950's* (Berkeley: University of California Press, 1998), p. 168.

[26]Ibid, p. 168.

[27]Douglas Wood, illustrated by Cheng-Khee Chee, *Old Turtle* (Duluth, Minnesota: Pheifer-Hamilton, 1992).

[28]Anonymous, *The Jerusalem Community Rule of Life* (Mahwah, New Jersey: Paulist Press, 1985), p. 8.

[29]Some useful books that describe what to expect from spiritual direction are: Chapter Two of my first book, *Romancing the Holy* (New York: Crossroad Publishing, 1997); Margaret Guenther, *Holy Listening: The Art of Spiritual Direction* (Boston: Cowley Publications, 1992), and Chapter Seven of Marjorie J. Thompson, *Soul Feast: An Invitation to the Christian Spiritual Life* (Louisville: Westminster John Knox Press, 1995).

[30]Flora Slosson Wuellner, *Prayer and Our Bodies* (Nashville: The Upper Room, 1987), p. 22.

[31]Ibid., p. 32.

[32]Anonymous, *The Rule of the Society of Saint John the Evangelist* (Boston: Cowley Publications, 1997), p. 88.

[33]John Cassian, Book 1, Chapter 3.

[34]Ibid, p. 30.

[35]Phil Porter with Cynthia Winton-Henry, *Having It All: Body, Mind,*

Heart & Spirit Together Again at Last (Oakland, California: Wing It! Press, 1997), p. 72ff.

[36]Ibid, p. 73.

[37]Anonymous, *The Jerusalem Community Rule of Life* (Mahwah, New Jersey: Paulist Press, 1985), p. 29.

[38]J. Philip Newell, *One Foot in Eden: A Celtic View of the Stages of Life* (Mahwah, New Jersey: Paulist Press, 1999), p. 63.

[39]C. H. Lawrence, *Medieval Monasticism: Forms of Religious Life in Western Europe in the Middle Ages* (London and New York: Longman, 1984), p. 28.

[40]Two popular books on the topic of voluntary simplicity, though not from a religious perspective, are: *Your Money or Your Life: Transforming Your Relationship with Money and Achieving Financial Independence*, Joe Dominguez and Vicki Robin (New York: Penguin, 1993), and Duane Elgin, *Voluntary Simplicity: Toward a Way of Life That Is Outwardly Simple, Inwardly Rich* (New York: Quill, 1993).

[41]I am indebted to L. William Countryman for this insight. In his book *Forgiven and Forgiving* (Harrisburg, Pennsylvania: Morehouse Publishing, 1998), Countryman talks about the process of forgiveness as one of conversion, of learning to see through God's eyes. This works equally well with the discipline of acceptance.

[42]Caroline Westerhoff, *Good Fences: The Boundaries of Hospitality* (Boston: Cowley Publications, 1999), p. 50.